POEMS
OF
THIS
CENTURY

EDITED BY

C. B. COX & A. E. DYSON

EDWARD ARNOLD

First published 1968
by Edward Arnold (Publishers) Ltd.
25 Hill Street, London W1X 8LL

Reprinted 1972

ISBN : 0 7131 1532 7

Printed in Great Britain by Cox & Wyman Ltd.,
London, Reading and Fakenham.

PREFACE

The editors of a school and college anthology have two possibilities open to them. They can choose poems which they judge suitable for a particular age-group, but would not put in an anthology designed for the world at large. Or they can choose poems which they consider excellent by any standards, but which also seem likely to appeal to the audience in view.

There is much to be said for both procedures, but we have favoured the second. Our aim has been to select poems that we have read and re-read over a long period, and think students will also enjoy. We have looked principally for poems by the best poets of the twentieth century, and while many very fine poems have been rejected on account of their difficulty, our hope is that the ones included will give as much pleasure to readers of this anthology as they have to ourselves.

It must be added, however, that the poems included are not altogether free from difficulties, including one difficulty which many very good poems present. To the question: 'What does it mean?' there is usually no simple answer. There may be two or more 'meanings', in single words, in images, lines or stanzas, perhaps in the poem as a whole. In our notes, we offer pointers to critical discussion, especially when double or multiple meanings are present, and draw attention to some of the suggestions and overtones that a simple paraphrase might miss. We try to give facts when these are needed, and to clear up difficulties of interpretation on specific points. But no detailed analyses of the poems are given, and in an anthology they would be out of place. We make observations which we hope will prove stimulating, and ask questions. (For readers wanting more, there are full analyses of some of these poems in our *Modern Poetry: Studies in Practical Criticism*, and a discussion of one of them—Ted Hughes's 'Six Young Men'—in our *The Practical Criticism of Poetry*.)

When readers are excited by any particular poet, we hope that they will look up his published volumes in a library, and start to browse. Very often, a liking for poetry starts in this way. On the first—or the third, or even the tenth—reading, a sudden delight may be felt. Perhaps this is because of what the poem *says*. We may recognize feelings or experiences familiar to us, but which we have never before had the right words to express; or we may be initiated to feelings and experiences that are altogether new. Or it may be the actual sounds and rhythms of the poem that delight us. They set up some inner resonance, and return later, in snatches or as a whole.

v

For every reader, the starting place may be different, but the better a poet is, the more likely he is to possess this power. We hope that all readers will find variety in this anthology, and some poems, at least, that they will not easily forget.

C. B. Cox
A. E. Dyson

CONTENTS

SECTION THREE

THE NEW POETRY

INTRODUCTION

Our anthology is divided into three sections of unequal length, the first called 'the early century', the second 'the modern', the third 'the new poetry'. These sections correspond approximately, but not exactly, to periods: 1900–1918, 1918–1945, and 1945 to the present day.

The poems chosen from the early century are meant as an introduction to the best that was being written before 'modern' poetry began. The poets were unaffected by the great changes in literature which defined themselves as 'modern', and still tended to think of poetry as set apart from everyday life. Their poetry reminds us of the joys of life (as in the poems of W. H. Davies printed here), or offers consolation for life's sorrow and pain. The poet's aim, they believed, was to celebrate beauty, and to create new beauty in his art.

Just before 1914, a number of poets began to emerge who rejected the idea that poetry should deal only with specially 'poetic' subjects and be chiefly notable for perfection of form. The most important innovators were Ezra Pound and T. S. Eliot. They asserted that the poet should return from his ivory tower to reality, and grapple with the whole range of modern life in the modern world. Their emphasis was on innovation and experiment. They chose new subjects—the industrial landscapes of modern living; the horror of modern war; the insights into human nature provided by evolutionary theory, psychology, political revolution; indeed, any themes important to our times. Almost necessarily, their poetry was experimental. The new themes could not be written about in the language and style appropriate to the old. Often they seem like prophets or evangelists, challenging the world to awaken from its sloth. As stylists, they reject clichés, generalizations, 'stock responses' in favour of the total living experience of the poet, dramatized in concrete words and images. 'Make it new', wrote Ezra Pound. Their most famous stylistic innovation was 'free-verse', which removes verse from carefully pre-scribed rules of rhyme and metre, and allows each poem to develop rhythms appropriate to itself. T. S. Eliot, Ezra Pound and D. H. Lawrence are the most notable 'free verse' poets—though each used 'freedom' in a very different way. The two giants of the 1920s and 1930s were T. S. Eliot and W. B. Yeats, the first an American who later became a naturalized Englishman, the second an Irishman born in 1865 who continued to develop as a poet until his death in 1939. During the winters from 1913 to 1915, Pound acted as Yeats's secretary, and was influential in changing

Yeats's style towards the modern. From this time on, the modern movement was supreme, both in America and Britain. Among the most important new American poets was Wallace Stevens, whose sophistications make him unsuitable for this anthology.

In the 1930s a number of young poets came on to the scene, mostly in their late teens or very early twenties. Four left-wing poets (W. H. Auden, Louis MacNeice, Stephen Spender, C. Day Lewis) introduced political themes into poetry, and tried to influence such important social events as mass unemployment, the struggle between Fascism and Communism, the Spanish War of 1937. And there was also Dylan Thomas, a wonderfully talented and exuberant young Welshman, whose poetry was written 'in praise of man and of God'.

Since 1945, poetry has again changed its direction. A number of major new poets have emerged who are most diverse in their views of poetry. In the 1950s, some of them were linked together by Robert Conquest as the 'Movement', and his anthology, *New Lines*, tried to formulate a common theory for their art. The most influential 'Movement' poet was Philip Larkin, who acknowledged the great importance to his own development of Thomas Hardy. The 'Movement' poets laid their stress on common experience, and accepted Wordsworth's view that a poet should be a man talking to men. They turned their backs on the larger endeavours and experiments of the 'moderns', and believed that poems should be compact, well-made, and readily intelligible in syntax and style.

But poets seldom adhere rigidly to the theories ascribed to them, and the two best 'Movement' poets, Philip Larkin and Thom Gunn, write very evocative, and sometimes mysterious, verse. Two of the best new poets of the 1950s, moreover, were wholly free from Movement influences and beliefs. These were Ted Hughes and R. S. Thomas—both very elemental poets, strong and austere in style and diction, whose explorations of man's bleak relationship to nature and the universe may stand as the major poetic achievement of recent times.

In the 1960s, the most striking poets to come into prominence have been Robert Lowell (an older American poet, whose full recognition has come comparatively late), and Sylvia Plath, a young American, the wife of Ted Hughes, who died tragically in 1963. These are sometimes called 'confessional' poets because they often use their personal life, including some very grim and frightening experiences, to explore the meaning of the modern world. In certain respects, they are more like the 'moderns' than most other recent poets are; they remind us that 'modern' poetry is still very relevant and alive.

We have included in our final section certain older poets who were never 'modern' in the sense defined here, and much of whose best work has been written since 1945. In addition to Robert Lowell (who has already been mentioned), the most notable ones are John Betjeman,

Edwin Muir and Robert Graves. This is a useful reminder that no living poet fits neatly into categories. D. H. Lawrence had many qualities in common with the poets of the early century, just as Edward Thomas and Wilfred Owen prefigured much that followed their death. We use our categories, therefore, to give shape to the anthology, and to underline the two main shifts in direction in this century, not to suggest rigid changes between one generation and the next. Critical distinctions are only scaffolding, to be removed when no longer useful, leaving the poem alone in splendour, entirely itself.

SECTION ONE
THE EARLY CENTURY

THE OLD VICARAGE, GRANTCHESTER

(Café des Westens, Berlin, May 1912)

Just now the lilac is in bloom,
All before my little room;
And in my flower-beds, I think,
Smile the carnation and the pink;
And down the borders, well I know,
The poppy and the pansy blow . . .
Oh! there the chestnuts, summer through,
Beside the river make for you
A tunnel of green gloom, and sleep
Deeply above; and green and deep
The stream mysterious glides beneath,
Green as a dream and deep as death.
—Oh, damn! I know it! and I know
How the May fields all golden show,
And when the day is young and sweet,
Gild gloriously the bare feet
That run to bathe . . .
                          Du lieber Gott!

Here am I, sweating, sick, and hot,
And there the shadowed waters fresh
Lean up to embrace the naked flesh.
Temperamentvoll German Jews
Drink beer around;—and *there* the dews
Are soft beneath a morn of gold.
Here tulips bloom as they are told;
Unkempt about those hedges blows
An English unofficial rose;
And there the unregulated sun
Slopes down to rest when day is done,
And wakes a vague unpunctual star,
A slippered Hesper; and there are
Meads towards Haslingfield and Coton
Where *das Betreten*'s not *verboten.*

7

Εἴθε γενοίμην ... would I were
In Grantchester, in Grantchester!—
Some, it may be, can get in touch
With Nature there, or Earth, or such.
And clever modern men have seen
A Faun a-peeping through the green,
And felt the Classics were not dead,
To glimpse a Naiad's reedy head,
Or hear the Goat-foot piping low: ...
But these are things I do not know.
I only know that you may lie
Day long and watch the Cambridge sky,
And, flower-lulled in sleepy grass,
Hear the cool lapse of hours pass,
Until the centuries blend and blur
In Grantchester, in Grantchester. ...
Still in the dawnlit waters cool
His ghostly Lordship swims his pool,
And tries the strokes, essays the tricks,
Long learnt on Hellespont, or Styx,
Dan Chaucer hears his river still
Chatter beneath a phantom mill.
Tennyson notes, with studious eye,
How Cambridge waters hurry by ...
And in that garden, black and white,
Creep whispers through the grass all night;
And spectral dance, before the dawn,
A hundred Vicars down the lawn;
Curates, long dust, will come and go
On lissom, clerical, printless toe;
And oft between the boughs is seen
The sly shade of a Rural Dean ...
Till, at a shiver in the skies,
Vanishing with Satanic cries,
The prim ecclesiastic rout
Leaves but a startled sleeper-out,
Grey heavens, the first bird's drowsy calls,
The falling house that never falls.

God! I will pack, and take a train,
And get me to England once again!
For England's the one land, I know,
Where men with Splendid Hearts may go;
And Cambridgeshire, of all England,
The shire for Men who Understand;
And of *that* district I prefer
The lovely hamlet Grantchester.
For Cambridge people rarely smile.
Being urban, squat, and packed with guile;
And Royston men in the far South
Are black and fierce and strange of mouth;
At Over they fling oaths at one,
And worse than oaths at Trumpington,
And Ditton girls are mean and dirty,
And there's none in Harston under thirty,
And folks in Shelford and those parts
Have twisted lips and twisted hearts,
And Barton men make Cockney rhymes,
And Coton's full of nameless crimes,
And things are done you'd not believe
At Madingley, on Christmas Eve.
Strong men have run for miles and miles,
When one from Cherry Hinton smiles;
Strong men have blanched, and shot their wives,
Rather than send them to St. Ives;
Strong men have cried like babes, bydam,
To hear what happened at Babraham.
But Grantchester! ah, Grantchester!
There's peace and holy quiet there,
Great clouds along pacific skies,
And men and women with straight eyes,
Lithe children lovelier than a dream,
A bosky wood, a slumbrous stream,
And little kindly winds that creep
Round twilight corners, half asleep.
In Grantchester their skins are white;
They bathe by day, they bathe by night;
The women there do all they ought;
The men observe the Rules of Thought.

They love the Good; they worship Truth;
They laugh uproariously in youth;
(And when they get to feeling old,
They up and shoot themselves, I'm told) . . .

Ah God! to see the branches stir
Across the moon at Grantchester!
To smell the thrilling-sweet and rotten
Unforgettable, unforgotten
River-smell, and hear the breeze
Sobbing in the little trees.
Say, do the elm-clumps greatly stand
Still guardians of that holy land?
The chestnuts shade, in reverend dream
The yet unacademic stream?
Is dawn a secret shy and cold
Anadyomene, silver-gold?
And sunset still a golden sea
From Haslingfield to Madingley?
And after, ere the night is born,
Do hares come out about the corn?
Oh, is the water sweet and cool,
Gentle and brown, above the pool?
And laughs the immortal river still
Under the mill, under the mill?
Say, is there Beauty yet to find?
And Certainty? and Quiet kind?
Deep meadows yet, for to forget
The lies, and truths, and pain? . . . oh! yet
Stands the Church clock at ten to three?
And is there honey still for tea?

Rupert Brooke

A GREAT TIME

Sweet Chance, that led my steps abroad,
  Beyond the town, where wild flowers grow—
A rainbow and a cuckoo, Lord,
  How rich and great the times are now!
    Know, all ye sheep
    And cows, that keep

On staring that I stand so long
  In grass that's wet from heavy rain—
A rainbow and a cuckoo's song
  May never come together again;
    May never come
    This side the tomb.

W. H. Davies

LEISURE

What is this life if, full of care,
We have no time to stand and stare.

No time to stand beneath the boughs
And stare as long as sheep or cows.

No time to see, when woods we pass,
Where squirrels hide their nuts in grass.

No time to see, in broad daylight,
Streams full of stars like skies at night.

No time to turn at Beauty's glance,
And watch her feet, how they can dance.

No time to wait till her mouth can
Enrich that smile her eyes began.

A poor life this if, full of care,
We have no time to stand and stare.

W. H. Davies

THE RAIN

I hear leaves drinking rain;
  I hear rich leaves on top
Giving the poor beneath
  Drop after drop;
'Tis a sweet noise to hear
These green leaves drinking near.

And when the Sun comes out,
  After this rain shall stop,
A wondrous light will fill
  Each dark, round drop;
I hope the Sun shines bright;
'Twill be a lovely sight.

W. H. Davies

THE LISTENERS

'Is there anybody there?' said the Traveller,
  Knocking on the moonlit door;
And his horse in the silence champed the grasses
  Of the forest's ferny floor:
And a bird flew up out of the turret,
  Above the Traveller's head:

And he smote upon the door again a second time;
  'Is there anybody there?' he said.
But no one descended to the Traveller;
  No head from the leaf-fringed sill
Leaned over and looked into his grey eyes,
  Where he stood perplexed and still.
But only a host of phantom listeners
  That dwelt in the lone house then
Stood listening in the quiet of the moonlight
  To that voice from the world of men:
Stood thronging the faint moonbeams on the dark stair,
  That goes down to the empty hall,
Hearkening in an air stirred and shaken
  By the lonely Traveller's call.
And he felt in his heart their strangeness,
  Their stillness answering his cry,
While his horse moved, cropping the dark turf
  'Neath the starred and leafy sky;
For he suddenly smote on the door, even
  Louder, and lifted his head:—
'Tell them I came, and no one answered,
  That I kept my word', he said.
Never the least stir made the listeners,
  Though every word he spake
Fell echoing through the shadowiness of the still house
  From the one man left awake:
Ay, they heard his foot upon the stirrup,
  And the sound of iron on stone,
And how the silence surged softly backward,
  When the plunging hoofs were gone.

Walter de la Mare

THEN

Twenty, forty, sixty, eighty,
  A hundred years ago,

All through the night with lantern bright
    The Watch trudged to and fro.
And little boys tucked snug abed
    Would wake from dreams to hear—
'Two o' the morning by the clock,
    And the stars a-shining clear!'
Or, when across the chimney-tops
    Screamed shrill a North-East gale,
A faint and shaken voice would shout,
    'Three!—and a storm of hail!'

Walter de la Mare

THE RAILWAY JUNCTION

From here through tunnelled gloom the track
Forks into two; and one of these
Wheels onward into darkening hills,
And one toward distant seas.

How still it is; the signal light
At set of sun shines palely green;
A thrush sings; other sound there's none,
Nor traveller to be seen—

Where late there was a throng. And now
In peace awhile, I sit alone;
Though soon, at the appointed hour,
I shall myself be gone.

But not their way: the bow-legged groom,
The parson in black, the widow and son,
The sailor with his cage, the gaunt
Gamekeeper with his gun,

That fair one, too, discreetly veiled—
All, who so mutely came, and went,

14

Will reach those far nocturnal hills,
Or shores, ere night is spent.

I nothing know why thus we met—
Their thoughts, their longings, hopes, their fate:
And what shall I remember, except—
The evening growing late—

That here through tunnelled gloom the track
Forks into two; of these
One into darkening hills leads on,
And one toward distant seas?

Walter de la Mare

THE OXEN

Christmas Eve, and twelve of the clock.
   'Now they are all on their knees',
An elder said as we sat in a flock
   By the embers in hearthside ease.

We pictured the meek mild creatures where
   They dwelt in their strawy pen,
Nor did it occur to one of us there
   To doubt they were kneeling then.

So fair a fancy few would weave
   In these years! Yet, I feel,
If someone said on Christmas Eve,
   'Come; see the oxen kneel

'In the lonely barton by yonder coomb
   Our childhood used to know',
I should go with him in the gloom,
   Hoping it might be so.

Thomas Hardy

15

AFTERWARDS

When the Present has latched its postern behind my tremulous stay,
   And the May month flaps its glad green leaves like wings,
Delicate-filmed as new-spun silk, will the neighbours say,
   'He was a man who used to notice such things'?

If it be in the dusk when, like an eyelid's soundless blink,
   The dewfall-hawk comes crossing the shades to alight
Upon the wind-warped upland thorn, a gazer may think,
   'To him this must have been a familiar sight.'

If I pass during some nocturnal blackness, mothy and warm,
   When the hedgehog travels furtively over the lawn,
One may say, 'He strove that such innocent creatures should come
   to no harm,
But he could do little for them; and now he is gone.'

If, when hearing that I have been stilled at last, they stand at the door,
   Watching the full-starred heavens that winter sees,
Will this thought rise on those who will meet my face no more,
   'He was one who had an eye for such mysteries'?

And will any say when my bell of quittance is heard in the gloom,
   And a crossing breeze cuts a pause in its outrollings,
Till they rise again, as they were a new bell's boom,
   'He hears it not now, but used to notice such things'?

Thomas Hardy

IN TIME OF 'THE BREAKING OF NATIONS'

Only a man harrowing clods
   In a slow silent walk
With an old horse that stumbles and nods
   Half asleep as they stalk.

Only thin smoke without flame
  From the heaps of couch-grass;
Yet this will go onward the same
  Though Dynasties pass.

Yonder a maid and her wight
  Come whispering by:
War's annals will cloud into night
  Ere their story die.

Thomas Hardy

STRANGE MEETING

It seemed that out of battle I escaped
Down some profound dull tunnel, long since scooped
Through granites which titanic wars had groined.
Yet also there encumbered sleepers groaned,
Too fast in thought or death to be bestirred.
Then, as I probed them, one sprang up, and stared
With piteous recognition in fixed eyes,
Lifting distressful hands as if to bless.
And by his smile, I knew that sullen hall,
By his dead smile I knew we stood in Hell.
With a thousand pains that vision's face was grained;
Yet no blood reached there from the upper ground,
And no guns thumped, or down the flues made moan.
'Strange friend', I said, 'here is no cause to mourn.'
'None', said the other, 'save the undone years,
The hopelessness. Whatever hope is yours,
Was my life also; I went hunting wild
After the wildest beauty in the world,
Which lies not calm in eyes, or braided hair,
But mocks the steady running of the hour,
And if it grieves, grieves richlier than here.
For by my glee might many men have laughed,
And of my weeping something had been left,
Which must die now. I mean the truth untold,

The pity of war, the pity war distilled.
Now men will go content with what we spoiled.
Or, discontent, boil bloody, and be spilled.
They will be swift with swiftness of the tigress,
None will break ranks, though nations trek from progress.
Courage was mine, and I had mystery;
Wisdom was mine, and I had mastery;
To miss the march of this retreating world
Into vain citadels that are not walled.
Then, when much blood had clogged their chariot-wheels
I would go up and wash them from sweet wells,
Even with truths that lie too deep for taint.
I would have poured my spirit without stint
But not through wounds; not on the cess of war.
Foreheads of men have bled where no wounds were.
I am the enemy you killed, my friend.
I knew you in this dark; for so you frowned
Yesterday through me as you jabbed and killed.
I parried; but my hands were loath and cold.
Let us sleep now. . . .'

Wilfred Owen

THE SEND-OFF

Down the close, darkening lanes they sang their way
To the siding-shed,
And lined the train with faces grimly gay.

Their breasts were stuck all white with wreath and spray
As men's are, dead.

Dull porters watched them, and a casual tramp
Stood staring hard,
Sorry to miss them from the upland camp.
Then, unmoved, signals nodded, and a lamp
Winked to the guard.

So secretly, like wrongs hushed-up, they went.
They were not ours:
We never heard to which front these were sent.

Nor there if they yet mock what women meant
Who gave them flowers.

Shall they return to beatings of great bells
In wild train-loads?
A few, a few, too few for drums and yells,
May creep back, silent, to village wells
Up half-known roads.

Wilfred Owen

DULCE ET DECORUM EST

Bent double, like old beggars under sacks,
Knock-kneed, coughing like hags, we cursed through sludge,
Till on the haunting flares we turned our backs,
And towards our distant rest began to trudge.
Men marched asleep. Many had lost their boots,
But limped on, blood-shod. All went lame, went blind;
Drunk with fatigue; deaf even to the hoots
Of gas-shells dropping softly behind.

Gas! GAS! Quick, boys!—an ecstasy of fumbling,
Fitting the clumsy helmets just in time,
But someone still was yelling out and stumbling
And floundering like a man in fire or lime.—
Dim through the misty panes and thick green light,
As under a green sea, I saw him drowning.

In all my dreams before my helpless sight
He plunges at me, guttering, choking, drowning.

If in some smothering dreams, you too could pace

Behind the wagon that we flung him in,
And watch the white eyes writhing in his face,
His hanging face, like a devil's sick of sin;
If you could hear, at every jolt, the blood
Come gargling from the froth-corrupted lungs,
Bitter as the cud
Of vile, incurable sores on innocent tongues,—
My friend, you would not tell with such high zest
To children ardent for some desperate glory,
The old Lie: Dulce et decorum est
Pro patria mori.

Wilfred Owen

FUTILITY

Move him into the sun—
Gently its touch awoke him once,
At home, whispering of fields unsown.
Always it woke him, even in France,
Until this morning and this snow.
If anything might rouse him now
The kind old sun will know.

Think how it wakes the seeds—
Woke, once, the clay of a cold star.
Are limbs, so dear-achieved, are sides,
Full-nerved—still warm—too hard to stir?
Was it for this the clay grew tall?
—O what made fatuous sunbeams toil
To break earth's sleep at all?

Wilfred Owen

EVERYONE SANG

Everyone suddenly burst out singing;
And I was filled with such delight
As prisoned birds must find in freedom,
Winging wildly across the white
Orchards and dark-green fields; on—on—and out of
    sight.

Everyone's voice was suddenly lifted;
And beauty came like the setting sun:
My heart was shaken with tears; and horror
Drifted away . . . O, but Everyone
Was a bird; and the song was wordless; the singing
    will never be done.

Siegfried Sassoon

OLD MAN

Old Man, or Lad's-love,—in the name there's nothing
To one that knows not Lad's-love, or Old Man,
The hoar-green feathery herb, almost a tree,
Growing with rosemary and lavender.
Even to one that knows it well, the names
Half decorate, half perplex, the thing it is:
At least, what that is clings not to the names
In spite of time. And yet I like the names.

The herb itself I like not, but for certain
I love it, as some day the child will love it
Who plucks a feather from the door-side bush
Whenever she goes in or out of the house.
Often she waits there, snipping the tips and shrivelling
The shreds at last on to the path, perhaps
Thinking, perhaps of nothing, till she sniffs

Her fingers and runs off. The bush is still
But half as tall as she, though it is as old;
So well she clips it. Not a word she says;
And I can only wonder how much hereafter
She will remember, with that bitter scent,
Of garden rows, and ancient damson trees
Topping a hedge, a bent path to a door,
A low thick bush beside the door, and me
Forbidding her to pick.
                                    As for myself,
Where first I met the bitter scent is lost.
I, too, often shrivel the grey shreds,
Sniff them and think and sniff again and try
Once more to think what it is I am remembering.
Always in vain. I cannot like the scent,
Yet I would rather give up others more sweet,
With no meaning, than this bitter one.
I have mislaid the key. I sniff the spray
And think of nothing; I see and I hear nothing;
Yet seem, too, to be listening, lying in wait
For what I should, yet never can, remember:
No garden appears, no path, no hoar-green bush
Of Lad's-love, or Old Man, no child beside,
Neither father nor mother, nor any playmate;
Only an avenue, dark, nameless, without end.

Edward Thomas

TWO PEWITS

Under the after-sunset sky
Two pewits sport and cry,
More white than is the moon on high
Riding the dark surge silently;
More black than earth. Their cry
Is the one sound under the sky.
They alone move, now low, now high,

And merrily they cry
To the mischievous Spring sky,
Plunging earthward, tossing high,
Over the ghost who wonders why
So merrily they cry and fly,
Nor choose 'twixt earth and sky,
While the moon's quarter silently
Rides, and earth rests as silently.

Edward Thomas

TALL NETTLES

Tall nettles cover up, as they have done
These many springs, the rusty harrow, the plough
Long worn out, and the roller made of stone:
Only the elm butt tops the nettles now.

This corner of the farmyard I like most:
As well as any bloom upon a flower
I like the dust on the nettles, never lost
Except to prove the sweetness of a shower.

Edward Thomas

THE MILL-POND

The sun blazed while the thunder yet
Added a boom:
A wagtail flickered bright over
The mill-pond's gloom:

Less than the cooing in the alder
Isles of the pool

Sounded the thunder through that plunge
Of waters cool.

Scared starlings on the aspen tip
Past the black mill
Outchattered the stream and the next roar
Far on the hill.

As my feet dangling teased the foam
That slid below
A girl came out. 'Take care!' she said—
Ages ago.

She startled me, standing quite close
Dressed all in white:
Ages ago I was angry till
She passed from sight.

Then the storm burst, and as I crouched
To shelter, how
Beautiful and kind, too, she seemed,
As she does now!

Edward Thomas

ADLESTROP

Yes. I remember Adlestrop—
The name, because one afternoon
Of heat the express-train drew up there
Unwontedly. It was late June.

The steam hissed. Someone cleared his throat.
No one left and no one came
On the bare platform. What I saw
Was Adlestrop—only the name

24

And willows, willow-herb, and grass,
And meadowsweet, and haycocks dry,
No whit less still and lonely fair
Than the high cloudlets in the sky.

And for that minute a blackbird sang
Close by, and round him, mistier,
Farther and farther, all the birds
Of Oxfordshire and Gloucestershire.

Edward Thomas

SECTION TWO

THE MODERN

LOOK, STRANGER...

Look, stranger, on this island now
The leaping light for your delight discovers,
Stand stable here
And silent be,
That through the channels of the ear
May wander like a river
The swaying sound of the sea.

Here at the small field's ending pause
When the chalk wall falls to the foam and its tall ledges
Oppose the pluck
And knock of the tide,
And the shingle scrambles after the sucking surf,
And the gull lodges
A moment on its sheer side.

Far off like floating seeds the ships
Diverge on urgent voluntary errands,
And the full view
Indeed may enter
And move in memory as now these clouds do,
That pass the harbour mirror
And all the summer through the water saunter.

W. H. Auden

LADY, WEEPING AT THE CROSSROADS

Lady, weeping at the crossroads,
Would you meet your love
In the twilight with his greyhounds,
And the hawk on his glove?

Bribe the birds then on the branches,
Bribe them to be dumb,
Stare the hot sun out of heaven
That the night may come.

Starless are the nights of travel,
Bleak the winter wind;
Run with terror all before you
And regret behind.

Run until you hear the ocean's
Everlasting cry;
Deep though it may be and bitter
You must drink it dry.

Wear out patience in the lowest
Dungeons of the sea,
Searching through the stranded shipwrecks
For the golden key.

Push on to the world's end, pay the
Dread guard with a kiss;
Cross the rotten bridge that totters
Over the abyss.

There stands the deserted castle
Ready to explore;
Enter, climb the marble staircase
Open the locked door.

Cross the silent empty ballroom,
Doubt and danger past;
Blow the cobwebs from the mirror
See yourself at last.

Put your hand behind the wainscot,
You have done your part;
Find the penknife there and plunge it
Into your false heart.

W. H. Auden

MUSÉE DES BEAUX ARTS

About suffering they were never wrong,
The Old Masters: how well they understood
Its human position; how it takes place
While someone else is eating or opening a window or
    just walking dully along;
How, when the aged are reverently, passionately waiting
For the miraculous birth, there always must be
Children who did not specially want it to happen, skating
On a pond at the edge of the wood:
They never forgot
That even the dreadful martyrdom must run its course
Anyhow in a corner, some untidy spot
Where the dogs go on with their doggy life and the
    torturer's horse
Scratches its innocent behind on a tree.

In Brueghel's *Icarus*, for instance: how everything
    turns away
Quite leisurely from the disaster; the ploughman may
Have heard the splash, the forsaken cry,
But for him it was not an important failure; the sun shone
As it had to on the white legs disappearing into the green
Water; and the expensive delicate ship that must have seen
Something amazing, a boy falling out of the sky,
Had somewhere to get to and sailed calmly on.

W. H. Auden

SAY THIS CITY HAS TEN MILLION SOULS

Say this city has ten million souls,
Some are living in mansions, some are living in holes:
Yet there's no place for us, my dear, yet there's no place for us.

Once we had a country and we thought it fair,
Look in the atlas and you'll find it there:
We cannot go there now, my dear, we cannot go there now.

In the village churchyard there grows an old yew,
Every spring it blossoms anew:
Old passports can't do that, my dear, old passports can't do that.

The consul banged the table and said:
'If you've got no passport you're officially dead':
But we are still alive, my dear, but we are still alive.

Went to a committee; they offered me a chair;
Asked me politely to return next year:
But where shall we go to-day, my dear, but where shall we go to-day?

Came to a public meeting; the speaker got up and said:
'If we let them in, they will steal our daily bread';
He was talking of you and me, my dear, he was talking of you and me.

Thought I heard the thunder rumbling in the sky;
It was Hitler over Europe, saying: 'They must die';
O we were in his mind, my dear, O we were in his mind.

Saw a poodle in a jacket fastened with a pin,
Saw a door opened and a cat let in:
But they weren't German Jews, my dear, but they weren't German Jews.

Went down the harbour and stood upon the quay,
Saw the fish swimming as if they were free:
Only ten feet away, my dear, only ten feet away.

Walked through a wood, saw the birds in the trees;
They had no politicians and sang at their ease:
They weren't the human race, my dear, they weren't the human race.

Dreamed I saw a building with a thousand floors,
A thousand windows and a thousand doors;
Not one of them was ours, my dear, not one of them was ours.

Stood on a great plain in the falling snow;
Ten thousand soldiers marched to and fro:
Looking for you and me, my dear, looking for you and me.

W. H. Auden

ANYONE LIVED IN A PRETTY HOW TOWN

anyone lived in a pretty how town
(with up so floating many bells down)
spring summer autumn winter
he sang his didn't he danced his did.

Women and men (both little and small)
cared for anyone not at all
they sowed their isn't they reaped their same
sun moon stars rain

children guessed (but only a few
and down they forgot as up they grew
autumn winter spring summer)
that noone loved him more by more

when by now and tree by leaf
she laughed his joy she cried his grief
bird by snow and stir by still
anyone's any was all to her

someones married their everyones
laughed their cryings and did their dance
(sleep wake hope and then) they
said their nevers they slept their dream

stars rain sun moon
(and only the snow can begin to explain
how children are apt to forget to remember
with up so floating many bells down)

one day anyone died i guess
(and noone stooped to kiss his face)
busy folk buried them side by side
little by little and was by was

all by all and deep by deep
and more by more they dream their sleep
noone and anyone earth by april
wish by spirit and if by yes.

Women and men (both dong and ding)
summer autumn winter spring
reaped their sowing and went their came
sun moon stars rain

E. E. Cummings

MOUSE

here's a little mouse)and
what does he think about, i
wonder as over this
floor(quietly with

bright eyes)drifts(nobody
can tell because
Nobody knows, or why
jerks Here &, here,
gr(oo)ving the room's Silence) this like
a littlest
poem a
(with wee ears and see?

tail frisks)
             (gonE)
  'mouse',

34

                    We are not the same you and
i, since here's a little he
or is
it It
?   (or was something we saw in the mirror)?

therefore we'll kiss; for maybe
what was Disappeared
into ourselves
who   (look).   ,startled

                                        E. E. Cummings

THE LOVE SONG OF J. ALFRED PRUFROCK

S'io credesse che mia risposta fosse
A persona che mai tornasse al mondo,
Questa fiamma staria senza piu scosse.
Ma perciocche giammai di questo fondo
Non torno vivo alcun, s'i'odo il vero,
Senza tema d'infamia ti rispondo.

Let us go then, you and I,
When the evening is spread out against the sky
Like a patient etherized upon a table;
Let us go, through certain half-deserted streets,
The muttering retreats
Of restless nights in one-night cheap hotels
And sawdust restaurants with oyster-shells:
Streets that follow like a tedious argument
Of insidious intent
To lead you to an overwhelming question . . .
Oh, do not ask, 'What is it?'
Let us go and make our visit.

In the room the women come and go
Talking of Michelangelo.

35

The yellow fog that rubs its back upon the window-panes,
The yellow smoke that rubs its muzzle on the window-panes,
Licked its tongue into the corners of the evening,
Lingered upon the pools that stand in drains,
Let fall upon its back the soot that falls from chimneys,
Slipped by the terrace, made a sudden leap,
And seeing that it was a soft October night,
Curled once about the house, and fell asleep.

And indeed there will be time
For the yellow smoke that slides along the street,
Rubbing its back upon the window-panes;
There will be time, there will be time
To prepare a face to meet the faces that you meet;
There will be time to murder and create,
And time for all the works and days of hands
That lift and drop a question on your plate;
Time for you and time for me,
And time yet for a hundred indecisions,
And for a hundred visions and revisions,
Before the taking of a toast and tea.

In the room the women come and go
Talking of Michelangelo.

And indeed there will be time
To wonder, 'Do I dare?' and, 'Do I dare?'
Time to turn back and descend the stair,
With a bald spot in the middle of my hair—
(They will say: 'How his hair is growing thin!')
My morning coat, my collar mounting firmly to the chin,
My necktie rich and modest, but asserted by a simple pin—
(They will say: 'But how his arms and legs are thin!')
Do I dare
Disturb the universe?
In a minute there is time
For decisions and revisions which a minute will reverse.

For I have known them all already, known them all—
Have known the evenings, mornings, afternoons,

I have measured out my life with coffee spoons;
I know the voices dying with a dying fall
Beneath the music from a farther room.
    So how should I presume?

And I have known the eyes already, known them all—
The eyes that fix you in a formulated phrase,
And when I am formulated, sprawling on a pin,
When I am pinned and wriggling on the wall,
Then how should I begin
To spit out all the butt-ends of my days and ways?
    And how should I presume?

And I have known the arms already, known them all—
Arms that are braceleted and white and bare
(But in the lamplight, downed with light brown hair!)
Is it perfume from a dress
That makes me so digress?
Arms that lie along a table, or wrap about a shawl.
    And should I then presume?
    And how should I begin?

              .   .   .   .   .

Shall I say, I have gone at dusk through narrow streets
And watched the smoke that rises from the pipes
Of lonely men in shirt sleeves, leaning out of windows? . . .

I should have been a pair of ragged claws
Scuttling across the floors of silent seas.

              .   .   .   .   .

And the afternoon, the evening, sleeps so peacefully!
Smoothed by long fingers,
Asleep . . . tired . . . or it malingers,
Stretched on the floor, here beside you and me.
Should I, after tea and cakes and ices,
Have the strength to force the moment to its crisis?
But though I have wept and fasted, wept and prayed,
Though I have seen my head (grown slightly bald)
        brought in upon a platter,

I am no prophet—and here's no great matter;
I have seen the moment of my greatness flicker,
And I have seen the eternal Footman hold my coat, and snicker,
And in short, I was afraid.

And would it have been worth it, after all,
After the cups, the marmalade, the tea,
Among the porcelain, among some talk of you and me,
Would it have been worth while,
To have bitten off the matter with a smile,
To have squeezed the universe into a ball
To roll it toward some overwhelming question,
To say; 'I am Lazarus, come from the dead,
Come back to tell you all, I shall tell you all'—
If one, settling a pillow by her head,
   Should say: 'That is not what I meant at all.
   That is not it, at all.'

And would it have been worth it, after all,
Would it have been worth while,
After the sunsets and the dooryards and the sprinkled streets,
After the novels, after the teacups, after the skirts that
   trail along the floor—
And this, and so much more?—
It is impossible to say just what I mean!
But as if a magic lantern threw the nerves in patterns on a
   screen:
Would it have been worth while
If one, settling a pillow or throwing off a shawl,
And turning toward the window, should say:
   'That is not it at all,
   That is not what I meant, at all.'

     .   .   .   .   .

No! I am not Prince Hamlet, nor was meant to be;
Am an attendant lord, one that will do
To swell a progress, start a scene or two,
Advise the prince; no doubt, an easy tool,
Deferential, glad to be of use,
Politic, cautious, and meticulous;

Full of high sentence, but a bit obtuse;
At times, indeed, almost ridiculous—
Almost, at times, the Fool.

I grow old . . . I grow old . . .
I shall wear the bottoms of my trousers rolled.

Shall I part my hair behind? Do I dare to eat a peach?
I shall wear white flannel trousers, and walk upon the beach.
I have heard the mermaids singing, each to each.

I do not think that they will sing to me.

I have seen them riding seaward on the waves
Combing the white hair of the waves blown back
When the wind blows the water white and black.

We have lingered in the chambers of the sea
By sea-girls wreathed with seaweed red and brown
Till human voices wake us, and we drown.

T. S. Eliot

PRELUDE

The winter evening settles down
With smell of steaks in passageways.
Six o'clock.
The burnt-out ends of smoky days.
And now a gusty shower wraps
The grimy scraps
Of withered leaves about your feet
And newspapers from vacant lots;
The showers beat
On broken blinds and chimney-pots,
And at the corner of the street
A lonely cab-horse steams and stamps.
And then the lighting of the lamps.

T. S. Eliot

JOURNEY OF THE MAGI

'A cold coming we had of it,
Just the worst time of the year
For a journey, and such a long journey:
The ways deep and the weather sharp,
The very dead of winter.'
And the camels galled, sore-footed, refractory,
Lying down in the melting snow.
There were times we regretted
The summer palaces on slopes, the terraces,
And the silken girls bringing sherbet.
Then the camel men cursing and grumbling
And running away, and wanting their liquor and women,
And the night-fires going out, and the lack of shelters,
And the cities hostile and the towns unfriendly
And the villages dirty and charging high prices:
A hard time we had of it.
At the end we preferred to travel all night,
Sleeping in snatches,
With the voices singing in our ears, saying
That this was all folly.

Then at dawn we came down to a temperate valley,
Wet, below the snow line, smelling of vegetation;
With a running stream and a water-mill beating the darkness,
And three trees on the low sky.
And an old white horse galloped away in the meadow.
Then we came to a tavern with vine-leaves over the lintel,
Six hands at an open door dicing for pieces of silver,
And feet kicking the empty wine-skins.
But there was no information, and so we continued
And arrived at evening, not a moment too soon
Finding the place; it was (you may say) satisfactory.

All this was a long time ago, I remember,
And I would do it again, but set down
This set down
This: were we led all that way for

Birth or Death? There was a Birth, certainly,
We had evidence and no doubt. I had seen birth and death,
But had thought they were different; this Birth was
Hard and bitter agony for us, like Death, our death.
We returned to our places, these Kingdoms,
But no longer at ease here, in the old dispensation,
With an alien people clutching their gods.
I should be glad of another death.

T. S. Eliot

AFTER APPLE-PICKING

My long two-pointed ladder's sticking through a tree
Toward heaven still,
And there's a barrel that I didn't fill
Beside it, and there may be two or three
Apples I didn't pick upon some bough.
But I am done with apple-picking now.
Essence of winter sleep is on the night,
The scent of apples: I am drowsing off.
I cannot rub the strangeness from my sight
I got from looking through a pane of glass
I skimmed this morning from the drinking trough
And held against the world of hoary grass.
It melted, and I let it fall and break.
But I was well
Upon my way to sleep before it fell,
And I could tell
What form my dreaming was about to take.
Magnified apples appear and disappear,
Stem end and blossom end,
And every fleck of russet showing clear.
My instep arch not only keeps the ache,
It keeps the pressure of a ladder-round.
I feel the ladder sway as the boughs bend.
And I keep hearing from the cellar bin

The rumbling sound
Of load on load of apples coming in.
For I have had too much
Of apple-picking: I am overtired
Of the great harvest I myself desired.
There were ten thousand thousand fruit to touch,
Cherish in hand, lift down, and not let fall.
For all
That struck the earth,
No matter if not bruised or spiked with stubble,
Went surely to the cider-apple heap
As of no worth.
One can see what will trouble
This sleep of mine, whatever sleep it is.
Were he not gone,
The woodchuck could say whether it's like his
Long sleep, as I describe its coming on,
Or just some human sleep.

Robert Frost

STOPPING BY WOODS ON A SNOWY EVENING

Whose woods these are I think I know.
His house is in the village though;
He will not see me stopping here
To watch his woods fill up with snow.

My little horse must think it queer
To stop without a farmhouse near
Between the woods and frozen lake
The darkest evening of the year.

He gives his harness bells a shake
To ask if there is some mistake.

The only other sound's the sweep
Of easy wind and downy flake.

The woods are lovely, dark and deep,
But I have promises to keep,
And miles to go before I sleep,
And miles to go before I sleep.

Robert Frost

THE BEST OF SCHOOL

The blinds are drawn because of the sun,
And the boys and the room in a colourless gloom
Of underwater float: bright ripples run
Across the walls as the blinds are blown
To let the sunlight in; and I,
As I sit on the shores of the class, alone,
Watch the boys in their summer blouses
As they write, their round heads busily bowed:
And one after another rouses
His face to look at me,
To ponder very quietly,
As seeing, he does not see.

And then he turns again, with a little, glad
Thrill of his work he turns again from me,
Having found what he wanted, having got what was to
        be had.

And very sweet it is, while the sunlight waves
In the ripening morning, to sit alone with the class
And feel the stream of awakening ripple and pass
From me to the boys, whose brightening souls it laves
For this little hour.

This morning, sweet it is
To feel the lads' looks light on me,
Then back in a swift, bright flutter to work;
Each one darting away with his
Discovery, like birds that steal and flee.

Touch after touch I feel on me
As their eyes glance at me for the grain
Of rigour they taste delightedly.
As tendrils reach out yearningly,
Slowly rotate till they touch the tree
That they cleave unto, and up which they climb
Up to their lives—so they to me.

I feel them cling and cleave to me
As vines going eagerly up; they twine
My life with other leaves, my time
Is hidden in theirs, their thrills are mine.

D. H. Lawrence

SNAKE

A snake came to my water-trough
On a hot, hot day, and I in pyjamas for the heat,
To drink there.

In the deep, strange-scented shade of the great dark carob-tree
I came down the steps with my pitcher
And must wait, must stand and wait, for there he was at the
    trough before me.

He reached down from a fissure in the earth-wall in the gloom
And trailed his yellow-brown slackness soft-bellied down,
    over the edge of the stone trough
And rested his throat upon the stone bottom,

And where the water had dripped from the tap, in a small clearness,
He sipped with his straight mouth,
Softly drank through his straight gums, into his slack long body,
Silently.

Someone was before me at my water-trough,
And I, like a second comer, waiting.

He lifted his head from his drinking, as cattle do,
And looked at me vaguely, as drinking cattle do,
And flickered his two-forked tongue from his lips, and mused a
     moment,
And stooped and drank a little more,
Being earth-brown, earth-golden from the burning bowels of the
     earth
On the day of Sicilian July, with Etna smoking.

The voice of my education said to me
He must be killed,
For in Sicily the black, black snakes are innocent, the gold are
     venomous.

And voices in me said, If you were a man
You would take a stick and break him now, and finish him off.

But must I confess how I liked him,
How glad I was he had come like a guest in quiet, to drink at my
     water-trough
And depart peaceful, pacified, and thankless,
Into the burning bowels of this earth?

Was it cowardice, that I dared not kill him?
Was it perversity, that I longed to talk to him?
Was it humility, to feel so honoured?
I felt so honoured.

And yet those voices:
If you were not afraid, you would kill him!

And truly I was afraid, I was most afraid,
But even so, honoured still more
That he should seek my hospitality
From out the dark door of the secret earth.

He drank enough
And lifted his head, dreamily, as one who has drunken,
And flickered his tongue like a forked night on the air, so black,
Seeming to lick his lips,
And looked around like a god, unseeing, into the air,
And slowly turned his head,
And slowly, very slowly, as if thrice adream,
Proceeded to draw his slow length curving round
And climb again the broken bank of my wall-face.

And as he put his head into that dreadful hole,
And as he slowly drew up, snake-easing his shoulders, and entered
    farther,
A sort of horror, a sort of protest against his withdrawing into that
    horrid black hole,
Deliberately going into the blackness, and slowly drawing himself
    after,
Overcame me now his back was turned.

I looked round, I put down my pitcher,
I picked up a clumsy log
And threw it at the water-trough with a clatter.

I think it did not hit him,
But suddenly that part of him that was left behind convulsed in
    undignified haste,
Writhed like lightning, and was gone
Into the black hole, the earth-lipped fissure in the wall-front,
At which, in the intense still noon, I stared with fascination.

And immediately I regretted it.
I thought how paltry, how vulgar, what a mean act!
I despised myself and the voices of my accursed human education.

And I thought of the albatross,
And I wished he would come back, my snake.

For he seemed to me again like a king,
Like a king in exile, uncrowned in the underworld,
Now due to be crowned again.

And so, I missed my chance with one of the lords
Of life.
And I have something to expiate;
A pettiness.

Taormina

D. H. Lawrence

MONEY-MADNESS

Money is our madness, our vast collective madness.

And of course, if the multitude is mad
the individual carries his own grain of insanity around with him.

I doubt if any man living hands out a pound note without a pang,
and a real tremor, if he hands out a ten-pound note.

We quail, money makes us quail.
It has got us down, we grovel before it in strange terror.
And no wonder, for money has a fearful cruel power among men.

But it is not money we are so terrified of,
it is the collective money-madness of mankind.
For mankind says with one voice: How much is he worth?
Has he no money? Then let him eat dirt, and go cold.—

And if I have no money, they will give me a little bread
so I do not die,
but they will make me eat dirt with it.
I shall have to eat dirt, I shall have to eat dirt
if I have no money.

It is that that I am frightened of.
And that fear can become a delirium.
It is fear of my money-mad fellow-men.

We must have some money
to save us from eating dirt.

And this is all wrong.

Bread should be free,
shelter should be free,
fire should be free
to all and anybody, all and anybody, all over the world.

We must regain our sanity about money
before we start killing one another about it.
It's one thing or the other.

D. H. Lawrence

THE SUNLIGHT ON THE GARDEN

The sunlight on the garden
Hardens and grows cold,
We cannot cage the minute
Within its nets of gold,
When all is told
We cannot beg for pardon.

Our freedom as free lances
Advances towards its end;
The earth compels, upon it
Sonnets and birds descend;
And soon, my friend,
We shall have no time for dances.

The sky was good for flying
Defying the church bells
And every evil iron
Siren and what it tells:
The earth compels,
We are dying, Egypt, dying

And not expecting pardon,
Hardened in heart anew,
But glad to have sat under
Thunder and rain with you,
And grateful too
For sunlight on the garden.

Louis MacNeice

PROGNOSIS

Goodbye, Winter,
The days are getting longer,
The tea-leaf in the teacup
Is herald of a stranger.

Will he bring me business
Or will he bring me gladness
Or will he come for cure
Of his own sickness?

With a pedlar's burden
Walking up the garden
Will he come to beg
Or will he come to bargain?

Will he come to pester,
To cringe or to bluster,
A promise in his palm
Or a gun in his holster?

Will his name be John
Or will his name be Jonah
Crying to repent
On the Island of Iona?

Will his name be Jason
Looking for a seaman
Or a mad crusader
Without rhyme or reason?

What will be his message—
War or work or marriage?
News as new as dawn
Or an old adage?

Will he give a champion
Answer to my question
Or will his words be dark
And his ways evasion?

Will his name be Love
And all his talk be crazy?
Or will his name be Death
And his message easy?

Louis MacNeice

SONG TO BE SUNG BY THE FATHER OF INFANT FEMALE CHILDREN

My heart leaps up when I behold
A rainbow in the sky;
Contrariwise, my blood runs cold
When little boys go by.
For little boys as little boys,
No special hate I carry,
But now and then they grow to men,

And when they do, they marry.
No matter how they tarry,
Eventually they marry.
And, swine among the pearls,
They marry little girls.

Oh, somewhere, somewhere, an infant plays,
With parents who feed and clothe him.
Their lips are sticky with pride and praise,
But I have begun to loathe him.
Yes, I loathe with a loathing shameless
This child who to me is nameless.
This bachelor child in his carriage
Gives never a thought to marriage,
But a person can hardly say knife
Before he will hunt him a wife.

I never see an infant (male),
A-sleeping in the sun,
Without I turn a trifle pale
And think, is *he* the one?
Oh, first he'll want to crop his curls,
And then he'll want a pony,
And then he'll think of pretty girls
And holy matrimony.
He'll put away his pony,
And sigh for matrimony.
A cat without a mouse
Is he without a spouse.

Oh, somewhere he bubbles bubbles of milk,
And quietly sucks his thumbs;
His cheeks are roses painted on silk,
And his teeth are tucked in his gums.
But alas, the teeth will begin to grow,
And the bubbles will cease to bubble;
Give a score of years or so,
The roses will turn to stubble.
He'll send a bond, or he'll write a book,
And his eyes will get that acquisitive look,

And raging and ravenous for the kill,
He'll boldly ask for the hand of Jill.
This infant whose middle
Is diapered still
Will want to marry
My daughter Jill.

Oh sweet be his slumber and moist his middle!
My dreams, I fear, are infanticiddle.
A fig for embryo Lohengrins!
I'll open all of his safety pins,
I'll pepper his powder and salt his bottle,
And give him readings from Aristotle,
Sand for his spinach I'll gladly bring,
And tabasco sauce for his teething ring,
And an elegant, elegant alligator
To play with in his perambulator.
Then perhaps he'll struggle through fire and water
To marry somebody else's daughter!

Ogden Nash

THIS IS GOING TO HURT JUST A LITTLE BIT

One thing I like less than most things is sitting in a dentist chair with
    my mouth wide open,
And that I will never have to do it again is a hope that I am against hope
    hopen.
Because some tortures are physical and some are mental,
But the one that is both is dental.
It is hard to be self-possessed
With your jaw digging into your chest,
So hard to retain your calm
When your fingernails are making serious alterations in your life line
    or love line or some other important line in your palm;
So hard to give your usual effect of cheery benignity

When you know your position is one of the two or three in life most
  lacking in dignity.
And your mouth is like a section of road that is being worked on,
And it is all cluttered up with stone crushers and concrete mixers and
  drills and steam rollers and there isn't a nerve in your head that
  you aren't being irked on.
Oh, some people are unfortunate enough to be strung up by thumbs,
And others have things done to their gums,
And your teeth are supposed to be being polished,
But you have reason to believe they are being demolished,
And the circumstance that adds most to your terror
Is that it's all done with a mirror,
Because the dentist may be a bear, or as the Romans used to say, only
  they were referring to a feminine bear when they said it, an ursa,
But all the same how can you be sure when he takes his crowbar in one
  hand and mirror in the other he won't get mixed up, the way you
  do when you try to tie a bow tie with the aid of a mirror, and forget
  that left is right and vice versa?
And then at last he says That will be all; but it isn't because he then coats
  your mouth from cellar to roof
With something that I suspect is generally used to put a shine on a
  horse's hoof,
And you totter to your feet and think, Well it's all over now and after
  all it was only this once,
And he says come back in three monce.
And this, O Fate, is I think the most vicious circle that thou ever sentest,
That Man has to go continually to the dentist to keep his teeth in good
  condition when the chief reason he wants his teeth in good condition
  is so that he won't have to go to the dentist.

Ogden Nash

THE RIVER-MERCHANT'S WIFE

A LETTER

While my hair was still cut straight across my forehead
I played about the front gate, pulling flowers.

You came by on bamboo stilts, playing horse,
You walked about my seat, playing with blue plums.
And we went on living in the village of Chokan:
Two small people, without dislike or suspicion.

At fourteen I married My Lord you.
I never laughed, being bashful.
Lowering my head, I looked at the wall.
Called to, a thousand times, I never looked back.

At fifteen I stopped scowling,
I desired my dust to be mingled with yours
For ever and for ever and for ever.
Why should I climb the look out?

At sixteen you departed,
You went into far Ku-to-yen, by the river of swirling eddies,
And you have been gone five months.
The monkeys make sorrowful noise overhead.

You dragged your feet when you went out.
By the gate now, the moss is grown, the different mosses,
Too deep to clear them away!
The leaves fall early this autumn, in wind.
The paired butterflies are already yellow with August
Over the grass in the West garden;
They hurt me. I grow older.
If you are coming down through the narrows of the river Kiang,
Please let me know beforehand,
And I will come out to meet you
                    As far as Cho-fu-Sa.

                                        By Rihaku

                                        Ezra Pound

THE PYLONS

The secret of these hills was stone, and cottages
Of that stone made,
And crumbling roads
That turned on sudden hidden villages.

Now over these small hills, they have built the concrete
That trails black wire;
Pylons, those pillars
Bare like nude giant girls that have no secret.

The valley with its gilt and evening look
And the green chestnut
Of customary root,
Are mocked dry like the parched bed of a brook.

But far above and far as sight endures
Like whips of anger
With lightning's danger
There runs the quick perspective of the future.

This dwarfs our emerald country by its trek
So tall with prophecy:
Dreaming of cities
Where often clouds shall lean their swan-white neck.

Stephen Spender

IN RAILWAY HALLS

In railway halls, on pavements near the traffic,
They beg, their eyes made big by empty staring
And only measuring Time, like the blank clock.

No, I shall weave no tracery of pen-ornament
To make them birds upon my singing-tree:
Time merely drives these lives which do not live
As tides push rotten stuff along the shore.

—There is no consolation, no, none,
In the curving beauty of that line
Traced on our graphs through History, where the oppressor
    Starves and deprives the poor.

Paint here no draped despairs, no saddening clouds
Where the soul rests, proclaims eternity.
But let the wrong cry out as raw as wounds
This time forgets and never heals, far less transcends.

Stephen Spender

THE LANDSCAPE NEAR AN AERODROME

More beautiful and soft than any moth
With burring furred antennae feeling its huge path
Through dusk, the air liner with shut-off engines
Glides over suburbs and the sleeves set trailing tall
To point the wind. Gently, broadly, she falls,
Scarcely disturbing charted currents of air.

Lulled by descent, the travellers across sea
And across feminine land indulging its easy limbs
In miles of softness, now let their eyes trained by watching
Penetrate through dusk the outskirts of this town
Here where industry shows a fraying edge.
Here they may see what is being done.

Beyond the winking masthead light
And the landing ground, they observe the outposts
Of work: chimneys like lank black fingers
Or figures, frightening and mad: and squat buildings

With their strange air behind trees, like women's faces
Shattered by grief. Here where few houses
Moan with faint light behind their blinds,
They remark the unhomely sense of complaint, like a dog
Shut out, and shivering at the foreign moon.

In the last sweep of love, they pass over fields
Behind the aerodrome, where boys play all day
Hacking dead grass: whose cries, like wild birds,
Settle upon the nearest roofs
But soon are hid under the loud city.

Then, as they land, they hear the tolling bell
Reaching across the landscape of hysteria,
To where, louder than all those batteries
And charcoaled towers against that dying sky,
Religion stands, the Church blocking the sun.

Stephen Spender

AN IRISH AIRMAN FORESEES HIS DEATH

I know that I shall meet my fate
Somewhere among the clouds above;
Those that I fight I do not hate,
Those that I guard I do not love;
My country is Kiltartan Cross,
My countrymen Kiltartan's poor,
No likely end could bring them loss
Or leave them happier than before.
Nor law, nor duty bade me fight,
Nor public men, nor cheering crowds,
A lonely impulse of delight
Drove to this tumult in the clouds;
I balanced all, brought all to mind,
The years to come seemed waste of breath,
A waste of breath the years behind
In balance with this life, this death.

W. B. Yeats

THE WILD SWANS AT COOLE

The trees are in their autumn beauty,
The woodland paths are dry,
Under the October twilight the water
Mirrors a still sky;
Upon the brimming water among the stones
Are nine-and-fifty swans.

The nineteenth autumn has come upon me
Since I first made my count;
I saw, before I had well finished,
All suddenly mount
And scatter wheeling in great broken rings
Upon their clamorous wings.

I have looked upon those brilliant creatures,
And now my heart is sore.
All's changed since I, hearing at twilight,
The first time on this shore,
The bell-beat of their wings above my head,
Trod with a lighter tread.

Unwearied still, lover by lover,
They paddle in the cold
Companionable streams or climb the air;
Their hearts have not grown old;
Passion or conquest, wander where they will,
Attend upon them still.

But now they drift on the still water,
Mysterious, beautiful;
Among what rushes will they build,
By what lake's edge or pool
Delight men's eyes when I awake some day
To find they have flown away?

W. B. Yeats

A PRAYER FOR MY DAUGHTER

Once more the storm is howling, and half hid
Under this cradle-hood and coverlid
My child sleeps on. There is no obstacle
But Gregory's wood and one bare hill
Whereby the haystack- and roof-levelling wind,
Bred on the Atlantic, can be stayed;
And for an hour I have walked and prayed
Because of the great gloom that is in my mind.

I have walked and prayed for this young child an hour
And heard the sea-wind scream upon the tower,
And under the arches of the bridge, and scream
In the elms above the flooded stream;
Imagining in excited reverie
That the future years had come,
Dancing to a frenzied drum,
Out of the murderous innocence of the sea.

May she be granted beauty and yet not
Beauty to make a stranger's eye distraught,
Or hers before a looking-glass, for such,
Being made beautiful overmuch,
Consider beauty a sufficient end,
Lose natural kindness and maybe
The heart-revealing intimacy
That chooses right, and never find a friend.

Helen being chosen found life flat and dull
And later had much trouble from a fool,
While that great Queen, that rose out of the spray,
Being fatherless could have her way
Yet chose a bandy-leggèd smith for man.
It's certain that fine women eat
A crazy salad with their meat
Whereby the Horn of Plenty is undone.

In courtesy I'd have her chiefly learned;
Hearts are not had as a gift but hearts are earned
By those that are not entirely beautiful;
Yet many, that have played the fool
For beauty's very self, has charm made wise,
And many a poor man that has roved,
Loved and thought himself beloved,
From a glad kindness cannot take his eyes.

May she become a flourishing hidden tree
That all her thoughts may like the linnet be,
And have no business but dispensing round
Their magnanimities of sound,
Nor but in merriment begin a chase,
Nor but in merriment a quarrel.
O may she live like some green laurel
Rooted in one dear perpetual place.

My mind, because the minds that I have loved,
The sort of beauty that I have approved,
Prosper but little, has dried up of late,
Yet knows that to be choked with hate
May well be of all evil chances chief.
If there's no hatred in a mind
Assault and battery of the wind
Can never tear the linnet from the leaf.

An intellectual hatred is the worst,
So let her think opinions are accursed.
Have I not seen the loveliest woman born
Out of the mouth of Plenty's horn,
Because of her opinionated mind
Barter that horn and every good
By quiet natures understood
For an old bellows full of angry wind?

Considering that, all hatred driven hence,
The soul recovers radical innocence
And learns at last that it is self-delighting,
Self-appeasing, self-affrighting,

And that its own sweet will is Heaven's will;
She can, though every face should scowl
And every windy quarter howl
Or every bellows burst, be happy still.

And may her bridegroom bring her to a house
Where all's accustomed, ceremonious;
For arrogance and hatred are the wares
Peddled in the thoroughfares.
How but in custom and in ceremony
Are innocence and beauty born?
Ceremony's a name for the rich horn,
And custom for the spreading laurel tree.

W. B. Yeats

WHAT THEN?

His chosen comrades thought at school
He must grow a famous man;
He thought the same and lived by rule,
All his twenties crammed with toil;
'What then?' sang Plato's ghost. 'What then?'

Everything he wrote was read,
After certain years he won
Sufficient money for his need,
Friends that have been friends indeed;
'What then?' sang Plato's ghost. 'What then?'

All his happier dreams came true—
A small old house, wife, daughter, son,
Grounds where plum and cabbage grew,
Poets and Wits about him drew;
'What then?' sang Plato's ghost. 'What then?'

'The work is done', grown old he thought,
'According to my boyish plan;
Let the fools rage, I swerved in naught,
Something to perfection brought';
But louder sang that ghost, 'What then?'

W. B. Yeats

FOR ANNE GREGORY

'Never shall a young man
Thrown into despair,
By those great honey-coloured
Ramparts at your ear,
Love you for yourself alone
And not your yellow hair.'

'But I can get a hair-dye
And set such colour there,
Brown, or black, or carrot,
That young men in despair
May love me for myself alone
And not my yellow hair.'

'I heard an old religious man
But yesternight declare
That he had found a text to prove
That only God, my dear,
Could love you for yourself alone
And not your yellow hair.'

W. B. Yeats

MAD AS THE MIST AND SNOW

Bolt and bar the shutter,
For the foul winds blow:
Our minds are at their best this night,
And I seem to know
That everything outside us is
Mad as the mist and snow.

Horace there by Homer stands,
Plato stands below,
And here is Tully's open page.
How many years ago
Were you and I unlettered lads
Mad as the mist and snow?

You ask what makes me sigh, old friend,
What makes me shudder so?
I shudder and I sigh to think
That even Cicero
And many-minded Homer were
Mad as the mist and snow.

W. B. Yeats

SECTION THREE

THE NEW POETRY

A LINCOLNSHIRE TALE

Kirkby with Muckby-cum-Sparrowby-cum-Spinx
Is down a long lane in the county of Lincs,
And often on Wednesdays, well-harnessed and spruce,
I would drive into Wiss over Winderby Sluice.

A whacking great sunset bathed level and drain
From Kirkby with Muckby to Beckby-on-Bain,
And I saw, as I journeyed, my marketing done,
Old Caistorby tower take the last of the sun.

The night air grew nippy. An autumn mist roll'd
(In a scent of dead cabbages) down from the wold,
In the ocean of silence that flooded me round
The crunch of the wheels was a comforting sound.

The lane lengthened narrowly into the night
With the Bain on its left bank, the drain on its right,
And feebly the carriage-lamps glimmered ahead
When all of a sudden *the pony fell dead.*

The remoteness was awful, the stillness intense,
Of invisible fenland, around and immense;
And out on the dark, with a roar and a swell,
Swung, hollowly thundering, Speckleby bell.

Though myself the Archdeacon for many a year,
I had not summoned courage for visiting here;
Our incumbents were mostly eccentric or sad
But—*the Speckleby Rector was said to be mad.*

Oh cold was the ev'ning and tall was the tower
And strangely compelling the tenor bell's power!
As loud on the reed-beds and strong through the dark
It toll'd from the church in the tenantless park.

The mansion was ruined, the empty demesne
Was slowly reverting to marshland again—

Marsh where the village was, grass in the Hall,
And the church and the Rectory waiting to fall.

And even in springtime with kingcups about
And stumps of old oak-trees attempting to sprout,
'Twas a sinister place, neither fenland nor wold,
And doubly forbidding in darkness and cold.

As down swung the tenor, a beacon of sound,
Over listening acres of waterlogged ground
I stood by the tombs to see pass and repass
The gleam of a taper, through clear leaded glass,

And such lighting of lights in the thunderous roar
The heart summoned courage to hand at the door;
I grated it open on scents I knew well,
The dry smell of damp rot, the hassocky smell.

What a forest of woodwork in ochres and grains
Unevenly doubled in diamonded panes,
And over the plaster, so textured with time,
Sweet discoloration of umber and lime!

The candles ensconced on each high panelled pew
Brought the caverns of brass-studded baize into view,
But the roof and its rafters were lost to the sight
As they soared to the dark of the Lincolnshire night:

And high from the chancel arch paused to look down
A sign-painter's beasts in their fight for the Crown,
While massive, impressive, and still as the grave
A three-decker pulpit frowned over the nave.

Shall I ever forget what a stillness was there
When the bell ceased its tolling and thinned on the air?
Then an opening door showed a long pair of hands
And the Rector himself in his gown and his bands.

. . . . . .

Such a fell Visitation I shall not forget,

Such a rush through the dark, that I rush through it yet,
And I pray, as the bells ring o'er fenland and hill,
That the Speckleby acres be tenantless still.

John Betjeman

VERGISSMEINICHT

Three weeks gone and the combatants gone,
returning over the nightmare ground
we found the place again, and found
the soldier sprawling in the sun.

The frowning barrel of his gun
overshadowing. As we came on
that day, he hit my tank with one
like the entry of a demon.

Look. Here in the gunpit spoil
the dishonoured picture of his girl
who has put: *Steffi. Vergissmeinicht*
in a copybook gothic script.

We see him almost with content
abased, and seeming to have paid
and mocked at by his own equipment
that's hard and good when he's decayed.

But she would weep to see today
how on his skin the swart flies move;
the dust upon the paper eye
and the burst stomach like a cave.

For here the lover and killer are mingled
who had one body and one heart.
And death who had the soldier singled
has done the lover mortal hurt.

Homs Tripolitania, 1943

Keith Douglas

ENFIDAVILLE

In the church fallen like dancers
lie the Virgin and St. Thérèse
on little pillows of dust.
The detonations of the last few days
tore down the ornamental plasters
shivered the hands of Christ.

The men and women who moved like candles
in and out of the houses and the streets
are all gone. The white houses are bare
black cages. No one is left to greet
the ghosts tugging at door-handles
opening doors that are not there.

Now the daylight coming in from the fields
like a labourer, tired and sad,
is peering about among the wreckage, goes
past some corners as though with averted head
not looking at the pain this town holds,
seeing no one move behind the windows.

But already they are coming back; to search
like ants, poking in the debris, finding in it
a bed or a piano and carrying it out.
Who would not love them at this minute?
I seem again to meet
The blue eyes of the images in the church.

Tunisia, 1943

Keith Douglas

SIGHTSEEING

Along the long wide temple wall
Extends a large and detailed painting.

A demon's head, its mouth square open,
Inside the mouth a room of people squatting.

Its fangs the polished pillars of the room,
The crimson carpet of the floor its tongue.

Inside this room a painting on the wall,
A demon's head, its mouth square open.

Inside the mouth a room of people squatting,
Their faces blank, the artist did not care.

Inside that room a painting on the wall,
A demon's head, its mouth square open.

Somewhere you are squatting, somewhere there.
Imagination, like the eyes that strain

Against the wall, is happily too weak
To number all the jaws there are to slip.

D. J. Enright

RACE

When I returned to my home town
believing that no one would care
who I was and what I thought
it was as if the people caught
an echo of me everywhere
they knew my story by my face
and I who am always alone
became a symbol of my race

Like every living Jew I have
in imagination seen
the gas-chamber the mass grave

the unknown body which was mine
and found in every German face
behind the mask the mark of Cain
I will not make their thoughts my own
by hating people for their race

VANITY

Be assured, the Dragon is not dead
But once more from the pools of peace
Shall rear his fabulous green head.

The flowers of innocence shall cease
And like a harp the wind shall roar
And the clouds shake an angry fleece.

'Here, here is certitude,' you swore,
'Below this lightning-blasted tree.
Where once it strikes, it strikes no more.

'Two lovers in one house agree.
The roof is tight, the walls unshaken.
As now, so must it always be.'

Such prophecies of joy awaken
The toad who dreams away the past
Under your hearth-stone, light forsaken,

Who knows that certitude at last
Must melt away in vanity—
No gate is fast, no door is fast—

That thunder bursts from the blue sky,
That gardens of the mind fall waste,
That fountains of the heart run dry.

Robert Graves

SHE TELLS HER LOVE WHILE HALF ASLEEP

She tells her love while half asleep,
  In the dark hours,
    With half-words whispered low:
As Earth stirs in her winter sleep
  And puts out grass and flowers
    Despite the snow,
    Despite the falling snow.

Robert Graves

LOVE WITHOUT HOPE

Love without hope, as when the young bird-catcher
Swept off his tall hat to the Squire's own daughter,
So let the imprisoned larks escape and fly
Singing about her head, as she rode by.

Robert Graves

BLACK JACKETS

In the silence that prolongs the span
Rawly of music when the record ends,
  The red-haired boy who drove a van
In weekday overalls but, like his friends,

  Wore cycle boots and jacket here
To suit the Sunday hangout he was in,
  Heard, as he stretched back from his beer,
Leather creak softly round his neck and chin.

Before him, on a coal-black sleeve
Remote exertion had lined, scratched, and burned
   Insignia that could not revive
The heroic fall or climb where they were earned.

On the other drinkers bent together,
Concocting selves for their impervious kit,
   He saw it as no more than leather
Which, taut across the shoulders grown to it,

Sent through the dimness of a bar
As sudden and anonymous hints of light
   As those that shipping give, that are
Now flickers in the Bay, now lost in night.

He stretched out like a cat, and rolled
The bitterish taste of beer upon his tongue,
   And listened to a joke being told:
The present was the things he stayed among.

If it was only loss he wore,
He wore it to assert, with fierce devotion,
   Complicity and nothing more.
He recollected his initiation,

And one especially of the rites.
For on his shoulders they had put tattoos:
   The group's name on the left, The Knights,
And on the right the slogan Born to Lose.

Thom Gunn

CONSIDERING THE SNAIL

The snail pushes through a green
night, for the grass is heavy
with water and meets over

the bright path he makes, where rain
has darkened the earth's dark. He
moves in a wood of desire,

pale antlers barely stirring
as he hunts. I cannot tell
What power is at work, drenched there
with purpose, knowing nothing.
What is a snail's fury? All
I think is that if later

I parted the blades above
the tunnel and saw the thin
trail of broken white across
litter, I would never have
imagined the slow passion
to that deliberate progress.

Thom Gunn

ST. MARTIN AND THE BEGGAR

Martin sat young upon his bed
A budding cenobite,
Said 'Though I hold the principles
Of Christian life be right,
I cannot grow from them alone,
I must go out to fight'.

He travelled hard, he travelled far,
The light began to fail.
'Is not this act of mine,' he said,
'A cowardly betrayal,
Should I not peg my nature down
With a religious nail?'

75

Wind scudded on the marshland,
And, dangling at his side,
His sword soon clattered under hail:
What could he do but ride?—
There was not shelter for a dog,
The garrison far ahead.

A ship that moves on darkness
He rode across the plain,
When a brawny beggar started up
Who pulled at his rein
And leant dripping with sweat and water
Upon the horse's mane.

He glared into Martin's eyes
With eyes more wild than bold;
His hair sent rivers down his spine;
Like a fowl plucked to be sold
His flesh was grey. Martin said—
'What, naked in this cold?

'I have no food to give you,
Money would be a joke'.
Pulling his new sword from the sheath
He took his soldier's cloak
And cut it in two equal parts
With a single stroke.

Grabbing one to his shoulders,
Pinning it with his chin,
The beggar dived into the dark,
And soaking to the skin
Martin went on slowly
Until he reached the inn.

One candle on the wooden table,
The food and drink were poor,
The woman hobbled off, he ate,
Then casually before
The table stood the beggar as
If he had used the door.

Now dry for hair and flesh had been
By warm airs fanned,
Still bare but round each muscled thigh
A single golden band,
His eyes now wild with love, he held
The half cloak in his hand.

'You recognized the human need
Including yours, because
You did not hesitate, my saint,
To cut your cloak across;
But never since that moment
Did you regret the loss.

'My enemies would have turned away,
My holy toadies would
Have given all the cloak and frozen
Conscious that they were good.
But you, being a saint of men,
Gave only what you could'.

St. Martin stretched his hand out
To offer from his plate,
But the beggar vanished, thinking food
Like cloaks is needless weight.
Pondering on the matter,
St. Martin bent and ate.

Thom Gunn

CHURNING DAY

A thick crust, coarse-grained as limestone rough-cast,
hardened gradually on top of the four crocks
that stood, large pottery bombs, in the small pantry.
After the hot brewery of gland, cud and udder
cool porous earthenware fermented the buttermilk

for churning day, when the hooped churn was scoured
with plumping kettles and the busy scrubber
echoed daintily on the seasoned wood.
It stood then, purified, on the flagged kitchen floor.

Out came the four crocks, spilled their heavy lip
of cream, their white insides, into the sterile churn.
The staff, like a great whisky muddler fashioned
in deal wood, was plunged in, the lid fitted.
My mother took first turn, set up rhythms
that slugged and thumped for hours. Arms ached.
Hands blistered. Cheeks and clothes were spattered
with flabby milk.

                    Where finally gold flecks
began to dance. They poured hot water then,
sterilized a birchwood-bowl
and little corrugated butter-spades.
Their short stroke quickened, suddenly
a yellow curd was weighting the churned up white,
heavy and rich, coagulated sunlight
that they fished, dripping, in a wide tin strainer,
heaped up like gilded gravel in the bowl.

The house would stink long after churning day,
acrid as a sulphur mine. The empty crocks
were ranged along the wall again, the butter
in soft printed slabs was piled on pantry shelves.
And in the house we moved with gravid ease,
our brains turned crystals full of clean deal churns,
the plash and gurgle of the sour-breathed milk,
the pat and slap of small spades on wet lumps.

Seamus Heaney

THE HORSES

I climbed through woods in the hour-before-dawn dark.
Evil air, a frost-making stillness,

Not a leaf, not a bird,—
A world cast in frost. I came out above the wood

Where my breath left tortuous statues in the iron light.
But the valleys were draining the darkness

Till the moorline—blackening dregs of the brightening
    grey—
Halved the sky ahead. And I saw the horses:

Huge in the dense grey—ten together—
Megalith-still. They breathed, making no move,

With draped manes and tilted hind-hooves,
Making no sound.

I passed: not one snorted or jerked its head.
Grey silent fragments

Of a grey silent world.

I listened in emptiness on the moor-ridge.
The curlew's tear turned its edge on the silence.

Slowly detail leafed from the darkness. Then the sun
Orange, red, red erupted

Silently, and splitting to its core tore and flung cloud,
Shook the gulf open, showed blue,

And the big planets hanging—.
I turned

Stumbling in the fever of a dream, down towards
The dark woods, from the kindling tops,

And came to the horses.
                    There, still they stood,
But now steaming and glistening under the flow of light,

Their draped stone manes, their tilted hind-hooves
Stirring under a thaw while all around them

The frost showed its fires. But still they made no sound.
Not one snorted or stamped,

Their hung heads patient as the horizons,
High over valleys, in the red levelling rays—

In din of the crowded streets, going among the years, the
          faces,
May I still meet my memory in so lonely a place

Between the streams and the red clouds, hearing curlews,
Hearing the horizons endure.

Ted Hughes

SIX YOUNG MEN

The celluloid of a photograph holds them well,—
Six young men, familiar to their friends.
Four decades that have faded and ochre-tinged
This photograph have not wrinkled the faces or the hands.
Though their cocked hats are not now fashionable,
Their shoes shine. One imparts an intimate smile,
One chews a grass, one lowers his eyes, bashful,
One is ridiculous with cocky pride—
Six months after this picture they were all dead.

All are trimmed for a Sunday jaunt. I know
That bilberried bank, that thick tree, that black wall,
Which are there yet and not changed. From where these sit
You hear the water of seven streams fall
To the roarer in the bottom, and through all
The leafy valley a rumouring of air go.
Pictured here, their expressions listen yet,
And still that valley has not changed its sound
Though their faces are four decades under the ground.

This one was shot in an attack and lay
Calling in the wire, then this one, his best friend,
Went out to bring him in and was shot too;
And this one, the very moment he was warned
From potting at tin-cans in no-man's-land,
Fell back dead with his rifle-sights shot away.
The rest, nobody knows what they came to,
But come to the worst they must have done, and held it
Closer than their hope; all were killed.

Here see a man's photograph,
The locket of a smile, turned overnight
Into the hospital of his mangled last
Agony and hours; see bundled in it
His mightier-than-a-man dead bulk and weight:
And on this one place which keeps him alive
(In his Sunday best) see fall war's worst
Thinkable flash and rending, onto his smile
Forty years rotting into soil.

That man's not more alive whom you confront
And shake by the hand, see hale, hear speak loud,
Than any of these six celluloid smiles are,
Nor prehistoric or fabulous beast more dead;
No thought so vivid as their smoking blood:
To regard this photograph might well dement,
Such contradictory permanent horrors here
Smile from the single exposure and shoulder out
One's own body from its instant and heat.

Ted Hughes

81

HAWK ROOSTING

I sit in the top of the wood, my eyes closed.
Inaction, no falsifying dream
Between my hooked head and hooked feet:
Or in sleep rehearse perfect kills and eat.

The convenience of the high trees!
The air's buoyancy and the sun's ray
Are of advantage to me;
And the earth's face upward for my inspection.

My feet are locked upon the rough bark.
It took the whole of Creation
To produce my foot, my each feather:
Now I hold Creation in my foot

Or fly up, and revolve it all slowly—
I kill where I please because it is all mine.
There is no sophistry in my body:
My manners are tearing off heads—

The allotment of death.
For the one path of my flight is direct
Through the bones of the living.
No arguments assert my right:

The sun is behind me.
Nothing has changed since I began.
My eye has permitted no change.
I am going to keep things like this.

Ted Hughes

VIEW OF A PIG

The pig lay on a barrow dead.
It weighed, they said, as much as three men.
Its eyes closed, pink white eyelashes.
Its trotters stuck straight out.

Such weight and thick pink bulk
Set in death seemed not just dead.
It was less than lifeless, further off.
It was like a sack of wheat.

I thumped it without feeling remorse.
One feels guilty insulting the dead,
Walking on graves. But this pig
Did not seem able to accuse.

It was too dead. Just so much
A poundage of lard and pork.
Its last dignity had entirely gone.
It was not a figure of fun.

Too dead now to pity.
To remember its life, din, stronghold
Of earthly pleasure as it had been,
Seemed a false effort, and off the point.

Too deadly factual. Its weight
Oppressed me—how could it be moved?
And the trouble of cutting it up!
The gash in its throat was shocking, but not pathetic.

Once I ran at a fair in the noise
To catch a greased piglet
That was faster and nimbler than a cat,
Its squeal was the rending of metal.

Pigs must have hot blood, they feel like ovens.
Their bite is worse than a horse's—

They chop a half-moon clean out.
They eat cinders, dead cats.

Distinctions and admirations such
As this one was long finished with.
I stared at it a long time. They were going to scald it,
Scald it and scour it like a doorstep.

Ted Hughes

MY SISTER JANE

And I say nothing—no, not a word
About our Jane. Haven't you heard?
She's a bird, a bird, a bird, a bird.
Oh it never would do to let folks know
My sister's nothing but a great big crow.

Each day (we daren't send her to school)
She pulls on stockings of thick blue wool
To make her pin crow legs look right,
Then fits a wig of curls on tight,
And dark spectacles—a huge pair
To cover her very crowy stare.
Oh it never would do to let folks know
My sister's nothing but a great big crow.

When visitors come she sits upright
(With her wings and her tail tucked out of sight.)
They think her queer but extremely polite.
Then when the visitors have gone
She whips out her wings and with her wig on
Whirls through the house at the height of your head—
Duck, duck, or she'll knock you dead.
Oh it never would do to let folks know
My sister's nothing but a great big crow.

At meals whatever she sees she'll stab it—
Because she's a crow and that's a crow habit.
My mother says 'Jane! Your manners! Please!'
Then she'll sit quietly on the cheese,
Or play the piano nicely by dancing on the keys—
Oh it never would do to let folks know
My sister's nothing but a great big crow.

Ted Hughes

MYXOMATOSIS

Caught in the centre of a soundless field
While hot inexplicable hours go by
What trap is this? Where were its teeth concealed?
You seem to ask.
            I make a sharp reply,
Then clean my stick. I'm glad I can't explain
Just in what jaws you were to suppurate:
You may have thought things would come right again
If you could only keep quite still and wait.

Philip Larkin

AT GRASS

The eye can hardly pick them out
From the cold shade they shelter in,
Till wind distresses tail and mane;
Then one crops grass, and moves about
—The other seeming to look on—
And stands anonymous again.

Yet fifteen years ago, perhaps

Two dozen distances sufficed
To fable them: faint afternoons
Of Cups and Stakes and Handicaps,
Whereby their names were artificed
To inlay faded, classic Junes—

Silks at the start: against the sky
Numbers and parasols: outside,
Squadrons of empty cars, and heat,
And littered grass: then the long cry
Hanging unhushed till it subside
To stop-press columns on the street.

Do memories plague their ears like flies?
They shake their heads. Dusk brims the shadows.
Summer by summer all stole away,
The starting-gates, the crowds and cries—
All but the unmolesting meadows.
Almanacked, their names live; they

Have slipped their names, and stand at ease,
Or gallop for what must be joy,
And not a field-glass sees them home,
Or curious stop-watch prophesies:
Only the groom, and the groom's boy,
With bridles in the evening come.

Philip Larkin

MCMXIV

Those long uneven lines
Standing as patiently
As if they were stretched outside
The Oval or Villa Park,
The crowns of hats, the sun
On moustached archaic faces

86

Grinning as if it were all
An August Bank Holiday lark;

And the shut shops, the bleached
Established names on the sunblinds,
The farthings and sovereigns,
And dark-clothed children at play
Called after kings and queens,
The tin advertisements
For cocoa and twist, and the pubs
Wide open all day;

And the countryside not caring:
The place-names all hazed over
With flowering grasses, and fields
Shadowing Domesday lines
Under wheat's restless silence;
The differently-dressed servants
With tiny rooms in huge houses,
The dust behind limousines;

Never such innocence,
Never before or since,
As changed itself to past
Without a word—the men
Leaving the gardens tidy,
The thousands of marriages
Lasting a little while longer:
Never such innocence again.

Philip Larkin

ALL DAY IT HAS RAINED...

All day it has rained, and we on the edge of the moors
Have sprawled in our bell-tents, moody and dull as boors,
Groundsheets and blankets spread on the muddy ground

And from the first grey wakening we have found
No refuge from the skirmishing fine rain
And the wind that made the canvas heave and flap
And the taut wet guy-ropes ravel out and snap.
All day the rain has glided, wave and mist and dream,
Drenching the gorse and heather, a gossamer stream
Too light to stir the acorns that suddenly
Snatched from their cups by the wind south-westerly
Pattered against the tent and our upturned dreaming faces.
And we stretched out, unbuttoning our braces,
Smoking a Woodbine, darning dirty socks,
Reading the Sunday papers—I saw a fox
And mentioned it in the note I scribbled home;—
And we talked of girls, and dropping bombs on Rome,
And thought of the quiet dead and the loud celebrities
Exhorting us to slaughter, and the herded refugees;
—Yet thought softly, morosely of them, and as indifferently
As of ourselves or those whom we
For years have loved, and will again
Tomorrow maybe love; but now it is the rain
Possesses us entirely, the twilight and the rain.

And I can remember nothing dearer or more to my heart
Than the children I watched in the woods on Saturday
Shaking down burning chestnuts for the schoolyard's merry play,
Or the shaggy patient dog who followed me
By Sheet and Steep and up the wooded scree
To the Shoulder o' Mutton where Edward Thomas brooded long
On death and beauty—till a bullet stopped his song.

Alun Lewis

WATER

It was a Maine lobster town—
each morning boatloads of hands
pushed off for granite
quarries on the islands,

and left dozens of bleak
white frame houses stuck
like oyster shells
on a hill of rock,

and below us, the sea lapped
the raw little match-stick
mazes of a weir,
where the fish for bait were trapped.

Remember? We sat on a slab of rock.
From this distance in time,
it seems the colour
of iris, rotting and turning purpler,

but it was only
the usual gray rock
turning the usual green
when drenched by the sea.

The sea drenched the rock
at our feet all day,
and kept tearing away
flake after flake.

One night you dreamed
you were a mermaid clinging to a wharf-pile,
and trying to pull
off the barnacles with your hands.

We wished our two souls
might return like gulls
to the rock. In the end,
the water was too cold for us.

Robert Lowell

THE HORSES

Barely a twelvemonth after
The seven days war that put the world to sleep,
Late in the evening the strange horses came.
By then we had made our covenant with silence,
But in the first few days it was so still
We listened to our breathing and were afraid.
On the second day
The radios failed; we turned the knobs; no answer.
On the third day a warship passed us, heading north,
Dead bodies piled on the deck. On the sixth day
A plane plunged over us into the sea. Thereafter
Nothing. The radios dumb;
And still they stand in corners of our kitchens,
And stand, perhaps, turned on, in a million rooms
All over the world. But now if they should speak,
If on a sudden they should speak again,
If on the stroke of noon a voice should speak,
We would not listen, we would not let it bring
That old bad world that swallowed its children quick
At one great gulp. We would not have it again.
Sometimes we think of the nations lying asleep,
Curled blindly in impenetrable sorrow,
And then the thought confounds us with its strangeness.

The tractors lie about our fields; at evening
They look like dank sea-monsters couched and waiting.
We leave them where they are and let them rust:
'They'll moulder away and be like other loam'.
We make our oxen drag our rusty ploughs,
Long laid aside. We have gone back
Far past our fathers' land.
                              And then, that evening
Late in the summer the strange horses came.
We heard a distant tapping on the road,
A deepening drumming; it stopped, went on again
And at the corner changed to hollow thunder.
We saw the heads

Like a wild wave charging and were afraid.
We had sold our horses in our fathers' time
To buy new tractors. Now they were strange to us
As fabulous steeds set on an ancient shield
Or illustrations in a book of knights.
We did not dare go near them. Yet they waited,
Stubborn and shy, as if they had been sent
By an old command to find our whereabouts
And that long-lost archaic companionship.
In the first moment we had never a thought
That they were creatures to be owned and used.
Among them were some half-a-dozen colts
Dropped in some wilderness of the broken world,
Yet new as if they had come from their own Eden.
Since then they have pulled our ploughs and borne our loads,
But that free servitude still can pierce our hearts.
Our life is changed; their coming our beginning.

Edwin Muir

WATERCOLOUR OF GRANTCHESTER MEADOWS

There, spring lambs jam the sheepfold. In air
Stilled, silvered as water in a glass
Nothing is big or far.
The small shrew chitters from its wilderness
Of grassheads and is heard.
Each thumb-size bird
Flits nimble-winged in thickets, and of good colour.

Cloudrack and owl-hollowed willows slanting over
The bland Granta double their white and green
World under the sheer water
And ride that flux at anchor, upside down.
The punter sinks his pole.
In Byron's pool
Cat-tails part where the tame cygnets steer.

It is a country on a nursery plate.
Spotted cows revolve their jaws and crop
Red clover or gnaw beetroot
Bellied on a nimbus of sun-glazed buttercup.
Hedging meadows of benign
Arcadian green
The blood-berried hawthorn hides its spines with white.

Droll, vegetarian, the water rat
Saws down a reed and swims from his limber grove,
While the students stroll or sit,
Hands laced, in a moony indolence of love—
Black-gowned, but unaware
How in such mild air
The owl shall stoop from his turret, the rat cry out.

Sylvia Plath

POINT SHIRLEY

From Water-Tower Hill to the brick prison
The shingle booms, bickering under
The sea's collapse.
Snowcakes break and welter. This year
The gritted wave leaps
The seawall and drops onto a bier
Of quahog chips,
Leaving a salty mash of ice to whiten

In my grandmother's sand yard. She is dead,
Whose laundry snapped and froze here, who
Kept house against
What the sluttish, rutted sea could do.
Squall waves once danced
Ship timbers in through the cellar window;

A thresh-tailed, lanced
Shark littered in the geranium bed—

Such collusion of mulish elements
She wore her broom straws to the nub.
Twenty years out
Of her hand, the house still hugs in each drab
Stucco socket
The purple egg-stones: from Great Head's knob
To the filled-in Gut
The sea in its cold gizzard ground those rounds.

Nobody wintering now behind
The planked-up windows where she set
Her wheat loaves
And apple cakes to cool. What is it
Survives, grieves
So, over this battered, obstinate spit
Of gravel? The waves'
Spewed relics clicker masses in the wind,

Grey waves the stub-necked eiders ride.
A labour of love, and that labour lost.
Steadily the sea
Eats at Point Shirley. She died blessed,
And I come by
Bones, bones only, pawed and tossed,
A dog-faced sea.
The sun sinks under Boston, bloody red.

I would get from these dry-papped stones
The milk your love instilled in them.
The black ducks dive.
And though your graciousness might stream,
And I contrive,
Grandmother, stones are nothing of home
To that spumiest dove.
Against both bar and tower the black sea runs.

Sylvia Plath

MUSHROOMS

Overnight, very
Whitely, discreetly,
Very quietly

Our toes, our noses
Take hold on the loam,
Acquire the air.

Nobody sees us,
Stops us, betrays us;
The small grains make room.

Soft fists insist on
Heaving the needles,
The leafy bedding,

Even the paving.
Our hammers, our rams,
Earless and eyeless,

Perfectly voiceless,
Widen the crannies,
Shoulder through holes. We

Diet on water,
On crumbs of shadow,
Bland-mannered, asking

Little or nothing.
So many of us!
So many of us!

We are shelves, we are
Tables, we are meek,
We are edible,

Nudgers and shovers

In spite of ourselves.
Our kind multiplies:

We shall by morning
Inherit the earth.
Our foot's in the door.

Sylvia Plath

YOUR ATTENTION PLEASE

The Polar DEW has just warned that
A nuclear rocket strike of
At least one thousand megatons
Has been launched by the enemy
Directly at our major cities.
This announcement will take
Two and a quarter minutes to make,
You therefore have a further
Eight and a quarter minutes
To comply with the shelter
Requirements published in the Civil
Defence Code—section Atomic Attack.
A specially shortened Mass
Will be broadcast at the end
Of this announcement—
Protestant and Jewish services
Will begin simultaneously—
Select your wavelength immediately
According to instructions
In the Defence Code. Do not
Take well-loved pets (including birds)
Into your shelter—they will consume
Fresh air. Leave the old and bed-
ridden, you can do nothing for them.
Remember to press the sealing
Switch when everyone is in

The shelter. Set the radiation
Aerial, turn on the geiger barometer.
Turn off your television now.
Turn off your radio immediately
The Services end. At the same time
Secure explosion plugs in the ears
Of each member of your family. Take
Down your plasma flasks. Give your children
The pills marked one and two
In the C.D. green container, then put
Them to bed. Do not break
The inside airlock seals until
The radiation All Clear shows
(Watch for the cuckoo in your
perspex panel), or your District
Touring Doctor rings your bell.
If before this, your air becomes
Exhausted or if any of your family
Is critically injured, administer
The capsules marked 'Valley Forge'
(Red pocket in No. 1 Survival Kit)
For painless death. (Catholics
Will have been instructed by their priests
What to do in this eventuality.)
This announcement is ending. Our President
Has already given orders for
Massive retaliation—it will be
Decisive. Some of us may die.
Remember, statistically
It is not likely to be you.
All flags are flying fully dressed
On Government buildings—the sun is shining.
Death is the least we have to fear.
We are all in the hands of God,
Whatever happens happens by His Will.
Now go quickly to your shelters.

Peter Porter

THE FAR FIELD

I

I dream of journeys repeatedly:
Of flying like a bat deep into a narrowing tunnel,
Of driving alone, without luggage, out a long peninsula,
The road lined with snow-laden second growth,
A fine dry snow ticking the windshield,
Alternate snow and sleet, no on-coming traffic,
And no lights behind, in the blurred side-mirror,
The road changing from glazed tarface to a rubble of stone,
Ending at last in a hopeless sand-rut,
Where the car stalls,
Churning in a snowdrift
Until the headlights darken.

II

At the field's end, in the corner missed by the mower,
Where the turf drops off into a grass-hidden culvert,
Haunt of the cat-bird, nesting-place of the field-mouse,
Not too far away from the ever-changing flower-dump,
Among the tin cans, tyres, rusted pipes, broken machinery—
One learned of the eternal;
And in the shrunken face of a dead rat, eaten by rain and ground-beetles
(I found it lying among the rubble of an old coal bin)
And the tom-cat, caught near the pheasant-run,
Its entrails strewn over the half-grown flowers,
Blasted to death by the night watchman.

I suffered for birds, for young rabbits caught in the mower,
My grief was not excessive.
For to come upon warblers in early May
Was to forget time and death:
How they filled the oriole's elm, a twittering restless cloud, all one
     morning,
And I watched and watched till my eyes blurred from the bird shapes,—
Cape May, Blackburnian, Cerulean,—
Moving, elusive as fish, fearless,
Hanging, bunched like young fruit, bending the end branches,

Still for a moment,
Then pitching away in half-flight,
Lighter than finches,
While the wrens bickered and sang in the half-green hedgerows,
And the flicker drummed from his dead tree in the chicken-yard.

—Or to lie naked in sand,
In the silted shallows of a slow river,
Fingering a shell,
Thinking:
Once I was something like this, mindless,
Or perhaps with another mind, less peculiar;
Or to sink down to the hips in a mossy quagmire;
Or, with skinny knees, to sit astride a wet log,
Believing:
I'll return again,
As a snake or a raucous bird,
Or, with luck, as a lion.

I learned not to fear infinity,
The far field, the windy cliffs of forever,
The dying of time in the white light of tomorrow,
The wheel turning away from itself,
The sprawl of the wave,
The on-coming water.

III

The river turns on itself,
The tree retreats into its own shadow.
I feel a weightless change, a moving forward
As of water quickening before a narrowing channel
When banks converge, and the wide river whitens;
Or when two rivers combine, the blue glacial torrent
And the yellowish-green from the mountainy upland,—
At first a swift rippling between rocks,
Then a long running over flat stones
Before descending to the alluvial plain,
To the clay banks, and the wild grapes hanging from the elmtrees,
The slightly trembling water

Dropping a fine yellow silt where the sun stays;
And the crabs bask near the edge,
The weedy edge, alive with small snakes and bloodsuckers,—

I have come to a still, but not a deep centre,
A point outside the glittering current;
My eyes stare at the bottom of a river,
At the irregular stones, iridiscent sandgrains,
My mind moves in more than one place,
In a country half-land, half-water.

I am renewed by death, thought of my death,
The dry scent of a dying garden in September,
The wind fanning the ash of a low fire.
What I love is near at hand,
Always, in earth and air.

IV

The lost self changes,
Turning toward the sea,
A sea-shape turning around,—
An old man with his feet before the fire,
In robes of green, in garments of adieu.

A man faced with his own immensity
Wakes all the waves, all their loose wandering fire.
The murmur of the absolute, the why
Of being born fails on his naked ears.
His spirit moves like monumental wind
That gentles on a sunny blue plateau.
He is the end of things, the final man.

All finite things reveal infinitude:
The mountain with its singular bright shade
Like the blue shine on freshly frozen snow,
The after-light upon ice-burdened pines;
Odour of basswood on a mountain-slope,
A scent beloved of bees;
Silence of water above a sunken tree:
The pure serene of memory in one man,—
A ripple widening from a single stone
Winding around the waters of the world.

Theodore Roethke

THE TROIKA

Troika, troika! The snow moon
whirls through the forest.

Where lamplight like a knife
gleams through a door, I see two greybeards bending.
They're playing chess, it seems. And then one rises
and stands in silence. Does he hear me passing?

Troika, troika! In the moonlight
his spirit hears my spirit passing.

I whip the horses on. The houses vanish.
The moon looks over fields
littered with debris. And there in trenches
the guardsmen stand, wind fluttering their rags.

And there were darker fields without a moon.
I walk across a field, bound on an errand.
The errand's forgotten—something depended on it.
A nightmare! I have lost my father's horses!

And then a white bird rises
and goes before me, hopping through the forest.

I held the bird—it vanished with a cry,
and on a branch a girl sat sideways, combing
her long black hair. The dew
shone on her lips; her breasts were white as roses.

Troika, troika! Three white horses,
a whip of silver, and my father's sleigh . . .

When morning breaks, the sea
gleams through the branches,
and the white bird, enchanted,
is flying through the world, across the sea.

Louis Simpson

THE REDWOODS

Mountains are moving, rivers
are hurrying. But we
are still.

We have the thoughts of giants—
clouds, and at night the stars.

And we have names—guttural, grotesque—
Hamet, Og—names with no syllables.

And perish, one by one, our roots
gnawed by the mice. And fall.

And are too slow for death, and change
to stone. Or else too quick,

like candles in a fire. Giants
are lonely. We have waited long

for someone. By our waiting, surely
there must be someone at whose touch

our boughs would bend; and hands
to gather us; a spirit

to whom we are light as the hawthorn tree.
O if there is a poet

let him come now! We stand at the Pacific
like great unmarried girls,

turning in our heads the stars and clouds,
considering whom to please.

Louis Simpson

MID-AUGUST AT SOURDOUGH MOUNTAIN LOOKOUT

Down valley a smoke haze
Three days heat, after five days rain
Pitch glows on the fir-cones
Across rocks and meadows
Swarms of new flies.

I cannot remember things I once read
A few friends, but they are in cities.
Drinking cold snow-water from a tin cup
Looking down for miles
Through high still air.

Gary Snyder

ABOVE PATE VALLEY

We finished clearing the last
Section of trail by noon,
High on the ridge-side
Two thousand feet above the creek—
Reached the pass, went on
Beyond the white pine groves,
Granite shoulders, to a small
Green meadow watered by the snow,
Edged with Aspen—sun
Straight high and blazing
But the air was cool.
Ate a cold fried trout in the
Trembling shadows. I spied
A glitter, and found a flake
Black volcanic glass—obsidian—
By a flower. Hands and knees
Pushing the Bear grass, thousands
Of arrowhead leavings over a

Hundred yards. Not one good
Head, just razor flakes
On a hill snowed all but summer,
A land of fat summer deer,
They came to camp. On their
Own trails. I followed my own
Trail here. Picked up the cold-drill,
Pick, singlejack, and sack
Of dynamite.
Ten thousand years.

Gary Snyder

TRAVELLING THROUGH THE DARK

Travelling through the dark I found a deer
dead on the edge of the Wilson River road.
It is usually best to roll them into the canyon:
that road is narrow; to swerve might make more dead.

By glow of the tail-light I stumbled back of the car
and stood by the heap, a doe, a recent killing;
she had stiffened already, almost cold.
I dragged her off; she was large in the belly.

My fingers touching her side brought me the reason—
her side was warm; her fawn lay there waiting,
alive, still, never to be born.
Beside that mountain road I hesitated.

The car aimed ahead its lowered parking lights;
under the hood purred the steady engine.
I stood in the glare of the warm exhaust turning red;
around our group I could hear the wilderness listen.

I thought hard for us all—my only swerving—
then pushed her over the edge into the river.

William Stafford

NO ORDINARY SUNDAY

No ordinary Sunday. First the light
Falling dead through dormitory windows blind
With fog; and then, at breakfast, every plate
Stained with the small, red cotton flower; and no
Sixpence for pocketmoney. Greatcoats, lined
By the right, marched from their pegs, with slow
Poppy fires smouldering in one lapel
To light us through the fallen cloud. Behind
That handkerchief sobbed the quick Sunday bell.

A granite cross, the school field underfoot,
Inaudible prayers, hymn-sheets that stirred
Too loudly in the hand. When hymns ran out,
Silence, like silt, lay round so wide and deep
It seemed that winter held its breath. We heard
Only the river talking in its sleep:
Until the bugler flexed his lips, and sound
Cutting the fog cleanly like a bird,
Circled and sang out over the bandaged ground.

Then, low voiced, the headmaster called the roll
Of those who could not answer; every name
Suffixed with honour—'double first', 'kept goal
For Cambridge'—and a death—in spitfires, tanks,
And ships torpedoed. At his call there came
Through the mist blond heroes in broad ranks
With rainbows struggling on their chests. Ahead
Of us, in strict step, as we idled home,
Marched the formations of the towering dead.

November again, and the bugles blown
In a tropical Holy Trinity,
The heroes today stand further off, grown
Smaller but distinct. They flash no medals, keep
No ranks: through *Last Post* and *Reveille*
Their chins loll on their chests, like birds asleep.
Only when the long, last note ascends

Upon the wings of kites, some two or three
Look up: and have the faces of my friends.

Jon Stallworthy

IN THE STREET OF THE FRUIT STALLS

Wicks balance flame, a dark dew falls
In the street of the fruit stalls.
Melon, guava, mandarin,
Pyramid-piled like cannon balls,
Glow red-hot, gold-hot, from within.

Dark children with a coin to spend
Enter the lantern's orbit; find
Melon, guava, mandarin—
The moon compacted to a rind,
The sun in a pitted skin.

They take it, break it open, let
A gold or silver fountain wet
Mouth, fingers, cheek, nose, chin:
Radiant as lanterns, they forget
The dark street I am standing in.

Jon Stallworthy

DO NOT GO GENTLE INTO THAT GOOD NIGHT

Do not go gentle into that good night,
Old age should burn and rave at close of day;
Rage, rage against the dying of the light.

Though wise men at their end know dark is right,
Because their words have forked no lightning they
Do not go gentle into that good night.

Good men, the last wave by, crying how bright
Their frail deeds might have danced in a green bay,
Rage, rage against the dying of the light.

Wild men who caught and sang the sun in flight,
And learn, too late, they grieved it on its way,
Do not go gentle into that good night.

Grave men, near death, who see with blinding sight
Blind eyes could blaze like meteors and be gay,
Rage, rage against the dying of the light.

And you, my father, there on the sad height,
Curse, bless, me now with your fierce tears, I pray.
Do not go gentle into that good night.
Rage, rage against the dying of the light.

Dylan Thomas

POEM IN OCTOBER

It was my thirtieth year to heaven
Woke to my hearing from harbour and neighbour wood
And the mussel pooled and the heron
Priested shore
The morning beckon
With water praying and call of seagull and rook
And the knock of sailing boats on the net webbed wall
Myself to set foot
That second
In the still sleeping town and set forth.

My birthday began with the water-
Birds and the birds of the winged trees flying my name
Above the farms and the white horses
And I rose
In rainy autumn

And walked abroad in a shower of all my days.
High tide and the heron dived when I took the road
  Over the border
   And the gates
 Of the town closed as the town awoke.

  A springful of larks in a rolling
Cloud and the roadside bushes brimming with whistling
 Blackbirds and the sun of October
   Summery
  On the hill's shoulder,
Here were fond climates and sweet singers suddenly
Come in the morning where I wandered and listened
  To the rain wringing
   Wind blow cold
 In the wood faraway under me.

  Pale rain over the dwindling harbour
And over the sea wet church the size of a snail
  With its horns through mist and the castle
   Brown as owls
  But all the gardens
Of spring and summer were blooming in the tall tales
Beyond the border and under the lark full cloud.
   There could I marvel
   My birthday
 Away but the weather turned around.

  It turned away from the blithe country
And down the other air and the blue altered sky
  Streamed again a wonder of summer
   With apples
  Pears and red currants
And I saw in the turning so clearly a child's
Forgotten mornings when he walked with his mother
  Through the parables
   Of sun light
 And the legends of the green chapels

  And the twice told fields of infancy

That his tears burned my cheeks and his heart moved in mine.
These were the woods the river and sea
Where a boy
In the listening
Summertime of the dead whispered the truth of his joy
To the trees and the stones and the fish in the tide.
And the mystery
Sang alive
Still in the water and singingbirds.

And there could I marvel my birthday
Away but the weather turned around. And the true
Joy of the long dead child sang burning
In the sun.
It was my thirtieth
Year to heaven stood there then in the summer noon
Though the town below lay leaved with October blood.
O may my heart's truth
Still be sung
On this high hill in a year's turning.

Dylan Thomas

FERN HILL

Now as I was young and easy under the apple boughs
About the lilting house and happy as the grass was green,
The night above the dingle starry,
Time let me hail and climb
Golden in the heydays of his eyes,
And honoured among wagons I was prince of the apple towns
And once below a time I lordly had the trees and leaves
Trail with daisies and barley
Down the rivers of the windfall light.

And as I was green and carefree, famous among the barns
About the happy yard and singing as the farm was home,

In the sun that is young once only,
    Time let me play and be
Golden in the mercy of his means,
And green and golden I was huntsman and herdsman, the calves
Sang to my horn, the foxes on the hills barked clear and cold,
    And the sabbath rang slowly,
    In the pebbles of the holy streams.

All the sun long it was running, it was lovely, the hay
Fields high as the house, the tunes from the chimneys, it was air
    And playing, lovely and watery
        And fire green as grass.
    And nightly under the simple stars
As I rode to sleep the owls were bearing the farm away,
All the moon long I heard, blessed among stables, the nightjars
    Flying with the ricks, and horses
        Flashing into the dark.

And then to awake, and the farm, like a wanderer white
With the dew, come back, the cock on his shoulder: it was all
    Shining, it was Adam and maiden,
        The sky gathered again
    And the sun grew round that very day.
So it must have been after the birth of the simple light
In the first, spinning place, the spellbound horses walking warm
    Out of the whinnying green stable
        On to the fields of praise.

And honoured among foxes and pheasants by the gay house
Under the new made clouds and happy as the heart was long
    In the sun born over and over,
        I ran my heedless ways,
    My wishes raced through the house high hay
And nothing I cared, at my sky blue trades, that time allows
In all his tuneful turning so few and such morning songs
    Before the children green and golden
        Follow him out of grace.

Nothing I cared, in the lamb white days, that time would take me
Up to the swallow thronged loft by the shadow of my hand,

In the moon that is always rising,
  Nor that riding to sleep
I should hear him fly with the high fields
And wake to the farm forever fled from the childless land.
Oh as I was young and easy in the mercy of his means,
  Time held me green and dying
Though I sang in my chains like the sea.

Dylan Thomas

ABERSOCH

There was that headland, asleep on the sea,
The air full of thunder and the far air
Brittle with lightning; there was that girl
Riding her cycle, hair at half-mast,
And the men smoking, the dinghies at rest
On the calm tide. There were people going
About their business, while the storm grew
Louder and nearer and did not break.

Why do I remember these few things,
That were rumours of life, not life itself
That was being lived fiercely, where the storm raged?
Was it just that the girl smiled,
Though not at me, and the men smoking
Had the look of those who have come safely home?

R. S. Thomas

A BLACKBIRD SINGING

It seems wrong that out of this bird,
Black, bold, a suggestion of dark
Places about it, there yet should come

Such rich music, as though the notes'
Ore were changed to a rare metal
At one touch of that bright bill.

You have heard it often, alone at your desk
In a green April, your mind drawn
Away from its work by sweet disturbance
Of the mild evening outside your room.

A slow singer, but loading each phrase
With history's overtones, love, joy
And grief learned by his dark tribe
In other orchards and passed on
Instinctively as they are now,
But fresh always with new tears.

R. S. Thomas

THE COUNTRY CLERGY

I see them working in old rectories
By the sun's light, by candlelight,
Venerable men, their black cloth
A little dusty, a little green
With holy mildew. And yet their skulls,
Ripening over so many prayers,
Toppled into the same grave
With oafs and yokels. They left no books,
Memorial to their lonely thought
In grey parishes; rather they wrote
On men's hearts and in the minds
Of young children sublime words
Too soon forgotten. God in his time
Or out of time will correct this.

R. S. Thomas

ON THE FARM

There was Dai Puw. He was no good.
They put him in the fields to dock swedes,
And took the knife from him, when he came home
At late evening with a grin
Like the slash of a knife on his face.

There was Llew Puw, and he was no good.
Every evening after the ploughing
With the big tractor he would sit in his chair,
And stare into the tangled fire garden,
Opening his slow lips like a snail.

There was Huw Puw, too. What shall I say?
I have heard him whistling in the hedges
On and on, as though winter
Would never again leave those fields,
And all the trees were deformed.

And lastly there was the girl:
Beauty under some spell of the beast.
Her pale face was the lantern
By which they read in life's dark book
The shrill sentence: God is love.

R. S. Thomas

SNOW SEQUENCE

A just-on-the-brink-of-snow feel,
a not-quite-real
access of late daylight. I tread
the puddles' hardness: rents
spread into yard-long splinters—
galactic explosions, outwards

from the stark, amoebic
shapes that air has pocketed
under ice. Even the sky
marbles to accord with grass
and frosted tree: the angles
of the world would be all knives, had not
the mist come up
to turn their edges,
just as the sun began
to slide from this precipice, this pause:
first flakes simultaneously
undid the stillness, scattering
across the disk
that hung, then dropped,
a collapsing bale-fire-red
behind the rimed, now snow-spanned
depth of a disappearing woodland.

Charles Tomlinson

ON THE DEATH OF A MURDERER

Over the hill the city lights leap up.
But there in the fields the quiet dusk folds down.
A man lies in a ditch. He listens hard.
His own fast breathing is the biggest sound
But through it, coming nearer, he hears another:
The voices of his hunters, coming nearer.

They are coming, and he can run no further.

He was born in a Germany thrashing like a fish
On a gravel towpath beating out its life.
As a child, something they called the Blockade
Nearly strangled him with impersonal cold fingers.

Clever doctors saved his life. The Blockade receded,
He hopped in the Berlin streets like a cool sparrow.
His wise friends showed him a quick way to earn
Pocket-money: while English schoolboys chalked
Dirty words and sniggered behind desk-lids,
He learnt the things the words meant; his pockets
Filled up with change and his heart jingled with hate.

Now his hate has jingled in the ears of Europe.
He has taught them to know the refusal of pity.
His life is nearly over; only the darkness
Covers him as his pursuers cry over the fields.
In a moment they will tear him to pieces.
He was sick of the things that went with the dirty words:
Sick of the pocket-money and the windy street.
Then the uniforms came. They said to him: *Be strong*

When he was fifteen, he had a gun.
He had forgotten the Blockade and the pocket-money,
Except on nights when he could not sleep: his gun
Was a friend, but when they gave him a whip
He loved that better still. *Be strong!* He cried.

The speeches were made, the leaves fell, it was war.
To smashed Prague his gun and his whip led him in time.
There, he learnt the delight of refusing pity.

Did he never wonder about those he murdered?
Never feel curious about the severe light
That flamed in their irises as they lay dying?
Apparently not. His duty took all his care.
He fed his starving heart with cruelty
Till it got sick and died. His masters applauded.
Once, he dragged off a man's lower jaw.

Now they are coming nearer over the fields.
It is like the Blockade, only worse. He will die.
They have taken away his whip and gun.

But let us watch the scene with a true eye,
Arrest your pen, hurrying chronicler.

Do you take this for a simple act: the mere
Crushing of a pest that crawled on the world's hide?
Look again: is there not an ironic light
In the fiery sky that rings his desperate head?

He will die, this cursed man. The first pursuer
Is here. The darkness is ready to give him up.
He has, at most, a hundred breaths to draw.
But what of the cunning devil that jerked his strings?
Is that one idle, now that the strings are cut?

The man's body will rot under lime, and that soon.
But the parades have taught his uniform to march.
The hunters close in: do they feel the danger?
When they wrench his body to pieces, will they hear
A sigh as his spirit is sucked into the air
That they must breathe? And will his uniform
March on, march on, across Europe? Will their children
Hop in the streets like cool sparrows, and draw
His spirit into their hopeful lungs? Will
Their hearts jingle with hate? And who shall save them
If after all the years and all the deaths
They find a world still pitiless, a street
Where no grass of love grows over the hard stones?

John Wain

THIS ABOVE ALL IS PRECIOUS AND REMARKABLE

This above all is precious and remarkable,
How we put ourselves in one another's care,
How in spite of everything we trust each other.

Fishermen at whatever point they are dipping and lifting
On the dark green swell they partly think of as home
Hear the gale warnings that fly to them like gulls.

The scientists study the weather for love of studying it,
And not specially for love of the fishermen,
And the wireless engineers do the transmission for love of wireless,

But how it adds up is that when the terrible white malice
Of the waves high as cliffs is let loose to seek a victim,
The fishermen are somewhere else and so not drowned.

And why should this chain of miracles be easier to believe
Than that my darling should come to me as naturally
As she trusts a restaurant not to poison her?

They are simply examples of well-known types of miracle,
The two of them,
That can happen at any time of the day or night.

John Wain

NOTES

RUPERT BROOKE (1887–1915) pp. 7–10.

Educated at Rugby and Cambridge. Died on way to take part in the Dardanelles expedition in 1915.

THE OLD VICARAGE, GRANTCHESTER. Grantchester is a short distance from Cambridge, along the River Cam. Brooke recalls its beauty, and his happiness as a boy there, and his present sense of exile. The rich nostalgia of this poem is famous, but note Rupert Brooke's precise images. His exclamation—'Oh, damn! I know it!'—conveys sharply his longing for home. In lines 21–32 he contrasts German neatness and bureaucracy with English freedom. There is a refreshing edge of prejudice (the poem was written in Berlin, two years before the First World War) and the adjectives–'unofficial' rose, 'unregulated' sun, 'vague unpunctual' star—point a witty defence of English ease, reinforced by the mocking use of German words and phrases. In lines 33–40 Brooke goes back to strong nostalgic feeling, tempered again by conversational good humour. He denies that he is a clever modern man. He recalls the many great men who have enjoyed the river in past centuries—Chaucer, Tennyson—as well as lesser men like himself. Lines such as 'The sly shade of a Rural Dean' continue the humour, which becomes more pronounced as Brooke champions Grantchester people against the other villagers of Cambridge-shire. The light-heartedness and innocence of this underline the poem's poignancy; it is as though the exile were already remembering home over a great distance, a paradise known only in myth. Brooke is still exaggerat-ing, and exaggerating outrageously, but behind his exaggeration is the truth he *feels*. The final lines (from 114 onwards) are more beautiful for the lightness of tone which has led up to them. There is still humour: 'yet unacademic stream' reminds us that the Cam at Grantchester has still to flow through Cambridge. In the final section, the poem personifies 'Beauty', 'Certainty' and 'Quiet' as qualities ineradically associated with the peaceful scene. The last two lines achieve a timeless quality, the distant but unchanging vividness of a child's afternoon.

Some critics have called this a 'sentimental' poem, and condemned it. What is your view? Do you think that 'sentimentality' is always bad? Is it necessarily bad here?

Do you feel a strong sense of the poet's personality behind the poem? The Greek phrase at the top of page 8 means 'would I were'. . .

Throughout these notes all poems which appear in this anthology are in small capitals.

W. H. DAVIES (1871–1940) pp. 11–12.

Born at Newport, Monmouthshire, of Welsh parents. Vagabond and tramp in England and America. From these experiences wrote *Autobiography of a Super-Tramp*. Successful as a writer post 1908.

If comment on these wonderful simple lyrics is superfluous, they are no less great than many of the more complicated poems in this book.

WALTER DE LA MARE (1873–1956) pp. 12–15.

Born in Kent. Educated at St. Paul's Cathedral Choir School. Eighteen years in service of the Standard Oil Company before devoting himself to literature. Short story-writer and novelist.

THE LISTENERS is a poem about silence and solitude. The Traveller arrives at his strange tryst to keep faith, but no one greets him. He rides off at the end still alone. The scene has an hypnotic clarity, as of meanings lurking just out of the reach of the conscious mind. The Traveller keeps faith, but with whom? The place, the people, remain shadowy. Is there anybody there? In the poem the Traveller asks, but receives no answer. What effect does his question have?

The other two poems of Walter de la Mare show his characteristic qualities—an evocation of vivid moments, long ago, far away, too strange for the space and time we ordinarily inhabit. Is THE RAILWAY JUNCTION a kind of allegory? de la Mare is particularly successful at creating a moment of loneliness and stillness. Would you describe these as sad poems?

THOMAS HARDY (1840–1928) pp. 15–17.

Born in Dorset. Educated at local school. Apprenticed to ecclesiastical architect. Major novelist. Fourteen novels published before 1895, when controversy over *Jude the Obscure* persuaded him to abandon fiction. Wrote poetry throughout his life.

THE OXEN at first seems a simple, almost childish, poem about the old superstition that oxen kneel down on Christmas Eve. But, when we look more closely, we may feel that its real subject is a comparison between Hardy's attitudes as child and adult. What do you think? Hardy is particularly successful in describing the passing of time, the mingling of past and present in the mind. What is he really saying in the last seven lines? In line 10, 'I feel' reduces the concluding lines to a fancy in his mind. The word 'gloom' in the penultimate line suggests the sadness in which he now lives. Is the last line as simple as it seems? How would you describe the quality of his 'hoping'?

Note how Hardy writes in an apparently archaic and contrived manner, with words such as 'barton' and 'coomb'. He inverts normal word order and uses alliteration—'So fair a fancy few would weave'. Many words might appear conventionally poetic—'embers', 'meek', 'mild', 'gloom'. And yet the poem is personal and intimate. If you count the syllables in each line, you will find noticeable variations from stanza to stanza. Lines such as 'Nor did it occur to one of us there' describe the children quite directly in natural, conversational language. This mixture of convention and originality suggests a contrast, perhaps, between the conventional beliefs of the child, and the personal loneliness of the adult poet?

In the other two Hardy poems note the exquisite response to twilight and dusk in AFTERWARDS and the care for simple common experiences in IN TIME OF 'THE BREAKING OF NATIONS'.

WILFRED OWEN (1893–1918) pp. 17–20.

Born in Oswestry. Educated at the Birkenhead Institute and the University of London. Killed in action, 1918, a few days before the Armistice.

STRANGE MEETING. 'My subject', wrote Owen, 'is war, and the pity of war. The poetry is in the pity.' His work marks a turning point in poetry written about the First World War, perhaps in all poetry about war. Owen is concerned not to glamorize fighting, but to expose its naked reality—young men squandered, whole nations engaged in a 'trek from progress'. For many people, the 1914–18 War was a time when progress ceased to seem the natural law of civilized life.

STRANGE MEETING tells of the encounter of a soldier just killed in battle with another soldier—an enemy—whom he had killed the day before. The scene is 'Hell', but it is more like the classical Hades than the Christian Hell. They meet in a twilight region, shadowy and joyless. The poem expresses, through the dead men's dialogue, the essence of pity—youthful love and achievement that *might* have been, forgiveness that comes too late. What force do you find in the line 'I am the enemy you killed, my friend'? And in the last line of the poem?

Note the poet's use of assonance and consonance (half-rhyme) instead of full rhyme, to suggest frustration and incompleteness. Formal beauty would be an evasion of war. 'The poetry is in the pity.' Owen directs attention away from his artistry to his theme.

THE SEND-OFF. In this poem, Owen describes the departure of young soldiers to battle. Again, he replaces the glamour often associated with such a moment with the shock of realism. The young men are sent off like cattle to the slaughter. Those who see them off are 'dull porters' and a 'casual tramp'. The cheering nation is not actually present. There is a suggestion that the soldiers go shamefully, as though they were criminals.

Does the nation transfer its own guilt to them, as to blood sacrifices? Most die obscurely, and those who survive slink back much later, as strangers and aliens. Owen remarkably prefigures the grudging reception afforded by post 1918 society to those of its 'heroes' who returned.

The imagery in this poem is concrete, yet mysterious. It is not wholly clear what a word like 'unmoved' (line 9) implies. What is your view? There is extraordinary power in the phrase 'They were not ours', and the quality of repudiation is all the stronger, perhaps, for not being defined.

DULCE ET DECORUM EST. Owen here is more nakedly savage. Consider the tone of the poem. The title derives from a famous phrase of the Latin poet Horace, 'It is sweet and fitting for a man to die for his country'. What is its force here?

FUTILITY. In this poem, about a soldier recently killed, Owen captures the quintessential folly of war.

SIEGFRIED SASSOON (1886–1967) p. 21.

Educated at Marlborough and Clare College, Cambridge. Served in 1914–18 War as infantry officer. Wrote autobiographical prose work, *The Complete Memoirs of George Sherston*, of which the first part, *Memoirs of a Fox-Hunting Man*, is particularly famous.

EVERYONE SANG. One of Sassoon's most well-known war poems, a sudden glimpse of heaven which lasts only a second amid all the horrors of war.

Would you describe it as a happy poem?

EDWARD THOMAS (1878–1917) pp. 21–25.

Educated at St. Paul's School and Oxford. Free-lance writer. Killed in 1914–18 War.

OLD MAN is one of the most difficult poems in this anthology. When we first read T. S. Eliot's PRUFROCK or THE WASTE LAND we may be bewildered by the jumbled scenes and the confusion of literary references, but Eliot's method is not too difficult to grasp. He is talking of people who have lost the will to act, who are in a condition of 'death-in-life'. Edward Thomas's vocabulary and descriptions are comparatively simple, but his experiences are not easy to understand. What is Thomas saying about this 'hoar-green feathery herb', which can be called either 'Old Man' or 'Lad's-love'?

One clue is found at the beginning of the second section, where Thomas says he does not *like* the herb but *loves* it. What is this love? The whole poem tries to define it. The herb is like life itself, stretching from lad's love to old age. It is bitter, unpleasant, so that the poet cannot say he *likes* it. But in all its mystery and tragedy, the herb may be loved, like life itself.

Another important clue is the word 'nothing', used in lines one, fifteen and thirty-four (twice). The plant suggests to Thomas (perhaps?) that behind human experiences there is nothing, no God, no final meaning. In the last four lines the garden disappears, and he sees only one picture— a dark, endless avenue, where humans travel without understanding where they are going or why. The avenue is nameless, because, as he says in the first lines, the names we give things can never be more than 'labels'. What does this suggest? Do you find it frightening?

This is a dark poem, but the central picture of the child has extraordinary beauty. Its 'meaning' lies a little beyond what our words (our names) can express.

TWO PEWITS is also difficult. The pewits, full of merriment and animation, are contrasted with the silence of moon and earth. The poet—the ghost—wonders at their energy. They are more black than earth, more white than the moon. What does this suggest to you? Why do you think the birds are said to be more white than moon, more black than earth? Why does Thomas expect them to choose between earth and sky? The energy of the pewits contrasts with the silence of earth and moon, and seems out of tune. Why does the poet call himself a ghost?

In TALL NETTLES, note the precision of detail. Thomas is not dreaming vaguely about the joys of days on the farm, but recording his experience exactly. We really believe him when he talks of the 'sweetness' of a shower.

THE MILL-POND records a moment of joy that is almost visionary. ADLESTROP also celebrates sudden delight, as if the poet steps wholly outside normal life.

W. H. AUDEN (1907–) pp. 29–33.

Born in York. Educated at Gresham's School, Holt, and Christ Church College, Oxford. At Oxford, 1925–28. Afterwards visited Berlin, taught in schools in England and Scotland, visited Iceland with Louis MacNeice, drove an ambulance for the Loyalists during the Spanish Civil War, and in 1938 visited China with Christopher Isherwood. January, 1939, went to live in United States, and became a U.S. citizen. Primarily a poet and critic.

LOOK, STRANGER, ON THIS ISLAND NOW shows Auden's love of alliteration and assonance, his splendid lyrical gift. In the last stanza, the wonderful landscape, the full view, move in the memory, becoming part of the mind like clouds reflected in water. Perhaps we are reminded of the island music of Shakespeare's *The Tempest?*

Auden is master of a variety of verse forms. LADY, WEEPING AT THE CROSSROADS adapts the ballad to a modern theme. The traditional themes of medieval romance—a weeping lady, a knight with hawk on glove and greyhounds, sinister landscapes, a journey to a deserted castle—are transformed into a story of betrayal and corruption. At the end of the quest, when the lady sees herself truly in the mirror, she recognizes that she is false. What does Auden suggest? Possibly that old standards of chivalry and honour have become debased?

MUSÉE DES BEAUX ARTS. Auden is looking at famous pictures in a gallery in Brussels, among them Brueghel's *Icarus*, described precisely in the last eight lines. Icarus, in Greek legend, flew too near the sun with wax wings, and fell as they melted. He is often used to represent human aspirations.

The poem's meaning at first seems simple. When great events take place, miracle or martyrdom, ordinary people continue with their everyday routines. But, in comparing the ordinary with the extraordinary, Auden is not so certain which is best. There is something ridiculous about the white legs disappearing into the green water. In line five, the aged people, reverently, passionately awaiting the miraculous birth, lack the spontaneity, vitality and innocence of the children. All the pictures of greatness—the miraculous birth, the martyrdom, the death of Icarus—are presented with a touch of ridicule. Is Auden perhaps suggesting that it is better to live an ordinary life than to suffer the spectacular fates of great men? Consider the tone of the word 'dreadful' in line 10. But, if we turn to the pictures of the commonplace, these too have more than one effect. Ordinary people may live contentedly, but they walk *dully* along; they are like dogs with their doggy lives, as ignoble as a horse scratching

its behind on a tree. Even the children seem menaced. Will the ice break?
What is hiding in the wood? The poem, written in the 1933–38 period,
suggests a conflict in Auden's mind. He detests the dullness of ordinary
life, yet fears heroic action. Can we afford heroes in the twentieth century?
But without heroes, what kind of a world would this be?

SAY THIS CITY HAS TEN MILLION SOULS. The extermination of millions
of German Jews by Hitler in the 1930s and early 1940s was the most
terrible crime of the century. Auden's poem is supposedly spoken by one
of the victims to his wife. What effect does the poem's rhythm have?
How far is this poem typical of the sufferings of 'modern man'? Do you
find any of the stanzas particularly bitter or challenging?

E. E. CUMMINGS (1894–1962) pp. 33–35.

Born in Cambridge, Mass. Educated at Harvard. Ambulance driver in
France during the First World War. Studied art in Paris, and lived as
poet and painter mainly in New York after 1924.

ANYONE LIVED IN A PRETTY HOW TOWN. The unusual language, at first
sight rather daunting, creates a mood of dreamlike gaiety. Most of the
lines cannot be paraphrased, but their meaning comes through vividly:
the man who 'sang his didn't' and 'danced his did' is surely a happy man?

The 'story' behind the poem seems simple. 'Anyone' is a man, 'noone'
a woman. They live, fall in love, know joy and sorrow, die and are buried.
'Women and men' in general care little what happens to these two, but
'he' and 'she' enact the full cycle of human love and grief. The poem's
mood is first idyllic then pathetic, but a dreamlike quality rules over
both. In the round of 'stars rain sun moon' anyone and noone count for
little, yet their lives are rich against this great backcloth, and their deaths
(stanza 7) are felt with tragic force. The final stanzas capture the transient
beauty of life as movingly as any poem in this collection. The gay, in-
consequential tone coexists with incantation and ritual. To describe the
full effect is impossible. Though the poem seems to float like an exquisite
bubble, iridescent and fragile, it is marvellously enduring—an image
of tragic compassion and of the wonder of life.

The other poem by E. E. Cummings enacts, through unorthodox
punctuation and odd effects of typography, a mouse's movements. It is
witty and compassionate, like much of his work.

T. S. ELIOT (1888–1965) pp. 35–41.

Born in St. Louis, Missouri. Studied at Harvard and Oxford. Left the
United States in 1914 and became British subject in 1927. Worked

as bank clerk for number of years, then as a publisher. Converted to Anglo-Catholic Church in late 1920s. Wrote many famous critical essays. Best known poems *The Waste Land* and *Four Quartets*; several plays, particularly *Murder in the Cathedral*.

THE LOVE SONG OF J. ALFRED PRUFROCK. This poem, full of allusions and evocative images, demands more explanation than can be offered here. See Northrop Frye's *T. S. Eliot* (Oliver and Boyd Writers and Critics series) for a general account, and Grover Smith's *T. S. Eliot's Poetry and Plays* (University of Chicago Phoenix book) for a detailed study of sources and meaning.

In this dramatic monologue, with its strong, almost incantatory rhythms, Prufrock is going one October evening to a tea-party where he will meet the woman he loves. He is no hero, however, and is even too timid to propose. Perhaps he represents all people who detest superficial society and question the meaning of life? But he is no prophet, and has not the courage to live out his ideas. A pathetic, frustrated man, he has been seen as typical of many people of his time, lost in a shadowy world, unsure about good and evil, afraid to act. What do you think?

The title and epigraph give some clues to the poem. The name 'J. Alfred Prufrock' suggests someone pompous, a little absurd. The epigraph is taken from Dante's *Inferno* XXVII, 61–66: 'If I thought my answer were to one who ever could return to the world, this flame (the damned soul) would shake (speak) no more; but since none ever did return alive from this depth, if what I hear be true, without fear of infamy I answer thee.' Guido da Montefeltro, tormented in the eighth circle of Hell for the sin of fraud through evil counsels, is answering Dante's question about his identity. His crime has been to pervert human reason by guile. Prufrock has similarly corrupted his reason, by timidity and inaction.

People have argued about the identity of 'you and I' in the first line. Is the reader 'you'? Or is Prufrock talking to himself? The comparison of an evening sun-set to a patient etherized upon a table was intended to shock the readers of the time, who were used to conventional praise of the beauties of Nature. How do you respond to it?

The city images of lines 3–12, and the fog (like a cat) of lines 15–25, suggest the emptiness and confusion of modern living. Prufrock feels impelled to ask an overwhelming question—what is the meaning of it all? But he finds it hard to face people. In lines 37–69 he mocks his fear of being laughed at, of breaking away from habit and routine. Under the eyes of the people he meets in society, he feels like an insect pinned on the wall, stuck-down by their certainty that they know exactly what he is like. In lines 70–74 he considers how little he has to offer. He could tell of his loneliness, walking the streets and looking at men in shirt-sleeves leaning out of windows, but what good would that do? It would perhaps have been better if he'd had the certainty of some crab-like creature, scuttling straight to its food across the ocean floor. The image is full of suggestions. What impression does this section of the poem make on you?

But Prufrock is not John the Baptist or Lazarus, reborn from the dead. He is not the confident lover of Andrew Marvell's poem 'To His Coy Mistress', from which words in line 92 are taken. He is too afraid, and too bored—'the afternoon, the evening, sleeps so peacefully'. If he could project his identity on to a screen, and show it to the lady (line 105), would it be worth it if she turned away and treated him with contempt? So his despair is not heroic, like that of Hamlet. He is more like Polonius —a Fool, a minor actor in the drama of life. Shall he part his hair behind to hide his baldness? Dare he eat a peach which may upset his stomach? The poem concludes with a beautiful dream-like image of mermaids and sea. In odd moments he has visions of wonder, hearing mermaids singing (the sirens?), seeing them ride the white foam of the waves, but their enchanted world is not for him. From drowning in such dreams of beauty he wakes to social reality, the boring tea-party, which is itself a 'drowning', a death-in-life. Does the ending seem in keeping with the poem?

PRELUDE is the first of four written between 1909 and 1911. The images create an atmosphere of gloom and frustration, partly by the choice of words—'burnt-out', 'smoky', 'grimy', 'withered', 'vacant', 'broken' and 'lonely'. 'Your feet' does not tell us whether the person is male or female; it is 'you', the reader, again, wrapped round by winter deadness, by meaningless newspapers. But note that these back-streets are not without some attraction for Eliot.

JOURNEY OF THE MAGI. 'Magi' means wise men—probably kings. One of the Magi, now an old man, recounts his journey to see the infant Christ (Matthew 2), and thinks about its meaning. The first section provides a vivid, realistic account of the journey. The opening quotation is taken from Lancelot Andrewes, an early seventeenth-century Anglican bishop. In the second section, the travellers move from winter to a temperate valley, and this foreshadows what Christ offers to the three kings— a rebirth. In the final section, the King thinks how Christ's birth was 'like Death, our death', for to see Christ was to die to their old selves and be born afresh. The poem concerns the whole meaning of Birth and Death ('three trees' recalls the crucifixion). Its matter-of-fact tone ('it was (you may say) satisfactory') links common experience with the wonders of Christ's birth. The king, among an alien people, is torn by doubt. What did it all mean, this great experience so long ago?

Try to define your own reaction to the poem. Would you have expected the Magi to feel like this? What attitude to them does the poem prompt us to take?

ROBERT FROST (1874–1963) pp. 41–43.

Born in San Francisco. After father's death when he was eleven, his mother brought him up in Lawrence, Massachusetts. Studied at Harvard, then tried teaching, newspaper work, shoemaking and farming. 1912–1915 in England, where made reputation as poet. Returned to U.S. to settle on a New Hampshire farm. Afterwards taught at several colleges and universities in the United States, including about twenty years at Amherst.

AFTER APPLE-PICKING. On first reading, this might seem just a vivid account of Frost's experiences as a farmer, with some fine evocations of his physical reactions—the ache in his instep arch from standing for hours on the ladder, the rumbling sound of the loads of apples. But is that all? The apple picker feels very much a part of seasonal change—autumn harvest turning towards winter, his work ending in sleep, his life ending in death. The ladder he works with points towards heaven. He recalls the strangeness of the grass seen through a piece of ice. He speaks with a sense of completeness, fulfilment—'Ripeness is all', as Shakespeare wrote in *King Lear*. The woodchuck has gone into hibernation; Frost reflects on his own dreams, on the sleep that is approaching 'whatever sleep it is'. In life in death, will be mysterious and satisfying after the wearying labours and satisfactions of this life. The symbolism is not lined in heavily, but delicately suggested. What are you personally reminded of?

STOPPING BY WOODS ON A SNOWY EVENING. This poem also uses a factual description—'And miles to go before I sleep'—to suggest a journey towards death. With their simple rhymes, rhythms and vocabulary, these verses are subtly resonant. Heavy-handed interpretation would be wrong. Frost has 'promises to keep' which conflict, it seems, with his pleasure in the woods—'lovely, dark and deep'. His delight in contemplating the woods fill up with snow seems an abandonment of his responsibilities, a mysterious involvement with the beautiful, cold world of death.

D. H. LAWRENCE (1885–1930) pp. 43–48.

Born in Eastwood, Nottinghamshire, son of coal-miner. Received teaching certificate from University College, Nottingham, and taught briefly at Croydon. Early experience very close to that of Paul Morel in his novel *Sons and Lovers* (1913). Rest of life devoted to writing fiction, also poetry, studies in psychology, and literary criticism. His nomadic life took him to Italy, Australia, the United States, and Mexico.

THE BEST OF SCHOOL shows Lawrence developing towards his mature use of free verse. This poem is rhymed, but length of line and rhythms are used freely to express Lawrence's relationship with his class. And 'the boys and the room in a colourless gloom Of underwater float' evokes not only the colour and quiet atmosphere, but suggests the boys lost in thought, occasionally, like the sunlight waves across the walls, awaking to semi-consciousness of the teacher, as they look up pondering. How far do the later sections of the poem depend on images of touch and growth? Lawrence feels the developing minds of the boys, alive, almost as if he can physically touch them. The tenderness and reverence for life, physically apprehended, is typical of Lawrence. With the boys, he is part of growth, like a tree surrounded by vines.

In SNAKE, the long lines mime the sinuous movement of the snake, while the short questions ('Was it cowardice, that I dared not kill him?') reflect the drama going on in Lawrence's mind. The earth-brown, earth-golden snake comes like an exiled king of the underworld, representing the mysterious forces of nature neglected by civilized man. After the poet has thrown the clumsy log, he feels ashamed, guilty. Why? Do you find this poem completely honest? What is your own feeling about snakes?

MONEY-MADNESS has a lively wit: 'I doubt if any man living hands out a pound note without a pang.' Lawrence's rhythms show the influence of the Authorized Version of the Bible. The repetition of 'madness', 'quail', 'money', 'bread', 'dirt', 'fear' and 'free' give the poem form and a symbolic force. Opponents of Lawrence would call these lines doggerel. What is your view?

LOUIS MACNEICE (1907–1963) pp. 48–50.

Born in Belfast, Ireland. Educated at Marlborough and Merton College, Oxford. University teacher, broadcaster and critic.

THE SUNLIGHT ON THE GARDEN is a love poem of the 1930s. The poet thinks that the end of normality, perhaps of civilization, is approaching. How does the opening image set the poem's tone?

MacNeice says that there is no appeal against reality. The 'freedom' of himself and other 'free-lance' artists is nearly over—poems return to earth, like birds, the dances finish. In stanza 3, aeroplane and siren are depicted as destroyers. The siren is probably a factory hooter, representing the tyranny of industry, but to readers who were alive in the Second World War (1939–45) it inevitably suggests the sirens which a few years after this poem was written warned of air-raids. The line 'We are dying, Egypt, dying' is spoken twice by the dying Antony in Shakespeare's *Antony and Cleopatra*, where political forces surround and destroy romantic love. In the last stanza the poet's heart is 'hardened' anew by these realities, but he still gives thanks for moments of happiness and affection.

Why does the poet's heart 'harden'? Does he harden it to ward off useless regret and self-pity? Or does he welcome sterner times? Consider the image implied by 'cage' used as a verb in line 3. What is the precise meaning of 'The earth compels', which appears twice? Note the intricate and unusual stanza structure. How would you describe the poem's rhyme scheme?

PROGNOSIS—a poem about the future. The tone is lilting and gay, but with a touch of stringency. From the almost casual opening, a reading of destiny in tea-leaves, the poet moves to a sufficiently serious conclusion. In the 1930s, change and war were imminent, and the poet does not expect one year to be like the last. There is exhilaration as well as danger in these many possibilities; the tea-leaves suggest nothing humdrum or routine. What is the effect of the poem's simple stanza form?

OGDEN NASH (1902–   ) pp. 50–53.

Born in Rye, N.Y. Educated at Newport, R.I., and Harvard.

SONG TO BE SUNG BY THE FATHER OF INFANT FEMALE CHILDREN. No comment. THIS IS GOING TO HURT JUST A LITTLE BIT ... Ditto.

EZRA POUND (1885–   ) pp. 53–54.

Born in Idaho. Educated at Hamilton College and University of Pennsylvania. Travelled and lived in Europe. Great influence on modern artists, particularly Yeats and T. S. Eliot. During 1939–45 War broadcast fascist propaganda from Rome. Imprisoned and adjudged insane after war. Kept in asylum in the United States until 1958.

THE RIVER-MERCHANT'S WIFE: A LETTER. One of Pound's early works, this poem lacks the difficulty of the later *Cantos*, the long work he has been writing for the last forty years. It is one of his 'creative' translations, apparently not very close to the original. Pound assumes a young Chinese woman's voice, imitating the way it had been imagined in the eighth century by Rihaku (the Japanese name for the poet, Li Po). He has an amazing ear for the music of words. How far does this Chinese girl of centuries ago seem to you like—or unlike—a young girl today?

STEPHEN SPENDER (1909–   ) pp. 55–57.

Educated at University College School, London, and Oxford. Associated with Auden, C. Day Lewis and MacNeice as one of left-wing political poets of the 1930s. In the Fire Service during 1939–45 War. Literary critic. Editor of *Encounter* for many years.

In THE PYLONS, Spender introduces modern inventions into poetry. The pylons carry the energy which will make the great cities of the future. But Spender's desire to celebrate modern technology is at war with his old-fashioned romantic love of Nature. The pylons are 'like whips of anger', suggesting cruelty, and the 'lightning's danger' is threatening. The pylons have no secrets, whereas the hills and cottages seem possessed of hidden sources of strength—the stone of the hills. Do you think the poet is excited by the pylons, or afraid of them?

IN RAILWAY HALLS . . . is about the poor during the terrible periods of unemployment of the 1930s. Spender insists that fine poetic phrases, 'tracery of pen-ornament', are inappropriate to this wrong. The poem shows the desire of the 1930s poets not to live in an ivory tower, but to become involved with the political and social problems of the time. Does it succeed?

THE LANDSCAPE NEAR AN AERODROME. This attack on modern industrial squalor puts before us two contrasted pictures. Examine the different ways in which Spender describes the aeroplane and the town. The aeroplane appears gentle, free, uninvolved in the mad hysteria of the town. Is the description of the aeroplane and its travellers entirely without adverse criticism?

W. B. YEATS (1865–1939) pp. 57–63.

Born in Dublin, Ireland, son of a painter. Supporter of Irish Nationalism, wrote and produced plays for Abbey Theatre in Dublin. Senator of Irish Free State from 1922–1928. But life mainly devoted to poetry.

AN IRISH AIRMAN FORESEES HIS DEATH was written in memory of Major Robert Gregory, son of Yeats's friend and patron, Lady Augusta Gregory. Gregory, an airman in the Royal Flying Corps, was killed on the Italian front in January 1918. Gregory does not believe that the fighting in the 1914–1918 War will help Ireland, and none of the normal reasons drove him to war—conscription, duty, political rhetoric, the cheers of the crowd. A hero, a man of balance, he prefers a moment of exaltation ('a lonely impulse of delight') to the commonplace activities of ordinary people. Note the use of 'balance' throughout the poem. Each line is carefully balanced with the next; this represents Gregory's triumph. He is a man of insight, who can balance a moment's glory with the waste of everyday life.

Many modern war poems are full of despair and disgust. Does Yeats admire Gregory?

THE WILD SWANS AT COOLE. Coole Park was the house of Lady Gregory, where Yeats passed many happy times. This is the first of three famous poems which he wrote about the estate—an emblem, to him, of all that was gracious and doomed. The swans are associated with the serene beauty of an aristocratic culture, and with its erosion and decay in the modern world. The 'fifty-nine' swans change, from year to year, but Yeats sees them as in some sense unchanging: it is himself, and the world, who move towards death. In the final stanza, he suggests that one day they will be gone for him, but other men may see them elsewhere.

As in many other poems, Yeats finds beauty revealed to men in time, but briefly and tantalizingly. Are the swans 'real' swans, or symbols?— or a little of each?

A PRAYER FOR MY DAUGHTER. In this poem, written in 1919, Yeats prays solemnly for his new-born daughter. The howling storm is an ominous reminder of the dangers surrounding human life. He prays that his daughter might have beauty, but not beauty so great that it would be a curse. What perils does he see in excessive beauty? 'Helen' is Helen of Troy, who eloped with the young Paris, betraying Menelaus her husband, and bringing about the Trojan war. The 'great Queen' is Aphrodite, the goddess of love, who is fabled to have risen from the ocean near Cyprus. 'A bandy-legged smith' is Hephaestus, the Greek god of fire and of the arts, such as that of the smith, in which fire is employed. The 'Horn of Plenty' is an image of the fountain of all blessings.

In stanza 5, Yeats prays that his daughter may have 'courtesy'. This is one of the great words of the poem. What does Yeats understand by it? The imagery of stanza 6 suggests perfect harmony and growth.

Stanzas 7 and 8 are more personal. The 'loveliest woman born' is Maud Gonne, whom Yeats had loved in vain for many years. Maud Gonne became involved in Irish politics, and after rejecting Yeats as a suitor she married John MacBride, a man whom Yeats thought of, as he says in 'Easter 1916', as 'a drunken, vainglorious lout'. Maud Gonne wasted her talents on political crusades, and her husband, who took part in the abortive Dublin rising of 1916, was put to death by the English as a traitor. Later, Yeats again proposed to Maud Gonne, and was again refused. This explains the very personal bitterness expressed in stanza 7. He asked Maud Gonne's permission to propose to her adopted daughter, Iseult, and having obtained permission, made his proposal, with no success. In October 1917 he married George Hyde-Lees (the mother of his daughter), and embarked on a life which proved, after an unhappy start, 'serene and full of order'.

The final two stanzas develop the idea that hatred is the enemy of human happiness, and state that true love is the one great blessing man can know. The final stanza, a prayer for his daughter's happiness in marriage in her adult life, is one of the most beautiful he ever wrote. His love of order, decency, ceremony and tradition, are nowhere more perfectly expressed than in the lines

> How but in custom and in ceremony
> Are innocence and beauty born?

WHAT THEN? The poem recounts a 'success story', with a sting in the tail. What is success? Plato is the great idealist philosopher of ancient Greece who testified to the necessary incompleteness of works wrought and achieved in time. All true, good, beautiful experiences point to ideal realities beyond the material world and mortal life. Yeats suggests that even a successful man, as the world knows success, becomes aware of incompleteness in his life and achievements. Plato's ghost has a permanent home in the human breast.

The colloquial phrase 'What Then?' suggests something light, and almost comic—is the ghost jeering? Is the joke wholly at the 'successful' man's expense?

FOR ANNE GREGORY. A delightful love poem, with more than a touch of Irish blarney. Essentially a lovers' dialogue, light and teasing, but with serious overtones. How far is 'beauty' a matter of physical attractiveness? *Can* anyone (except God) love another person for himself (or herself) alone? The poem's form derives from the ballad. As a witty dialogue—or pseudo-dialogue—it may remind us of love poems by Donne.

MAD AS THE MIST AND SNOW. A ballad not unlike WHAT THEN? in its implications, but less explicit—the images are elemental, the poem *suggests* rather than *states*. Horace, Homer, Plato, Tully, Cicero represent the great classical tradition of reason and human wisdom. On a wild night, even they are surrounded by mystery. The poem's refrain turns a wild night into an image of human experience. The poet and his friend, their minds 'at their best this night', still know as little of the essential mysteries of life as they did when 'unlettered lads'. The final stanza produces the shudder it speaks of by putting even the great masters of reason beyond reason's writ.

JOHN BETJEMAN (1906–   ) pp. 67–69.

Educated at Marlborough and Oxford. Has been schoolmaster, journalist, television celebrity. Great interest in English architecture, particularly of nineteenth century.

A LINCOLNSHIRE TALE. Note Betjeman's sensitivity to English landscape and architecture in this macabre story of the Lincolnshire fens. From the beginning there is deliberate exaggeration, a mock-melodramatic quality typical of Betjeman. The scene is 'strangely compelling', 'chill', 'forbidding', yet there is a sane gaiety in the bantering style. What, in your view, is the effect of a line such as 'A whacking great sunset bathed level and drain' (line 5)? Is the poem as simple as its striking rhymes and rhythms suggest?

KEITH DOUGLAS (1920–1944) pp. 69–70.

Born at Tunbridge Wells. Educated at Christ's Hospital, and Merton College, Oxford. Fought in a Crusader tank from Alamein to Tunisia; killed in Normandy, 1944. His *Alamein to Zem Zem* is a great prose account of tank warfare in the desert.

The German's body sprawls beside the photograph of his girl, with its simple message—Vergissmeinicht (Don't forget me). VERGISSMEINICHT records the full horror of death. But the images—the 'demon', 'the paper eye', the 'stomach like a cave'—distance the scene as if it were on a stage. There is a deliberately formal quality in the inversion in the opening line ('Three weeks gone'), in words such as 'weep', and in the solemn rhythms. All this invests death with a kind of ceremony and dignity. In *Alamein to Zem Zem*, Douglas writes: 'The most impressive thing about the dead is their triumphant silence, proof against anything in the world.' What is his attitude to death, in your opinion?

In ENFIDAVILLE Douglas recreates the wasted landscapes of war. Compare these two poems with the poems of Wilfred Owen. Do you find any notable similarities or differences between the two poets?

D. J. ENRIGHT (1920–   ) pp. 70–71.

Educated at Leamington College, and Downing College, Cambridge. Teacher of English Literature in many overseas countries. Novelist.

SIGHTSEEING. Most of us have been intrigued by some variation of this puzzle: if two mirrors face each other, where do the reflections end? Both our eye and our imagination can follow only a certain way—a happy weakness, says the poet. His image of a roomful of people 'squatting' inside a demon's mouth would be disconcerting even without the infinite repetition and recession, as in mirrors. The poem is elegant and sparse, with a throw-away wit that adds its own sting. It is a poem about a picture which contains its reader... and swallows him. Are we really there in the room? How many jaws, indeed?

KAREN GERSHON (1923–   ) pp. 71–72.

Jewish, born in Germany. Sent to England in 1938, leaving behind parents who died during the war.

RACE. A moving and personal poem, written by a German Jew who escaped from the Nazi persecutions of the 1930s. She revisits her home town, hoping to be anonymous, but finds herself a symbol of her race. In the second stanza, she acknowledges her destiny, but meets hatred with forgiveness. The ancient law of revenge 'an eye for an eye, a tooth for a tooth', is rejected. What moral view is adopted?

Note the flat tone, the unpunctuated sentences. It is as though all the 'natural' emotions of hatred are reined in.

ROBERT GRAVES (1895–   ) pp. 72–73.

Born in London. Educated at Charterhouse and Oxford. Infantry officer in the 1914–18 War. War experiences described in *Goodbye To All That*. Novelist, critic, and historian. Has lived in Majorca since 1929.

The title VANITY recalls the Old Testament words about the vanity of human wishes. There is a quality of nightmare in the images, which fade into each other, suggesting hidden dangers and the flavour of decay. Human hopes of love, fidelity, certainty, all crumble. The 'toad' is a reminder of Satan in Milton's *Paradise Lost*, 'squat like a toad', whispering infections into Eve's dreams. The 'Dragon', menacing but exotic, presides over the poem, which is bleak, pessimistic, but not colourless. What do you understand by the last three lines? The poem opens with an explosive imperative: 'Be assured...' Is the poet addressing the reader? How should the poem be read aloud?

The two short lyrics need little comment. No modern poet has written more exquisitely of love.

133

THOM GUNN (1929–) pp. 73–77.

Educated at Trinity College, Cambridge, and Stanford, California University teacher and freelance.

BLACK JACKETS is about a leather-jacketed boy in a café. His black jacket is the uniform of a 'set', but he stands apart from his fellows. There is the suggestion that he is more realistic; the others dream of exploits to fit their 'kit', but this boy prefers to live in the present. His main desire is 'complicity'—that is, the desire to belong to the set. The word 'initiation' underlines this; many secret societies have initiation rites.

The last stanza suggests two alternative ways of viewing the boys. Are they really heroic, the genuine descendants of the medieval knights? Or are they mere daydreamers, as the self-pitying slogan 'Born to Lose' seems to hint? Does the poet sympathize with the boys? Judge them? Or perhaps both?

Would you think from the third stanza that the boy's jacket once belonged to someone else, and that he still has to earn the right to it? The first image in the poem describes the moment between one record and the next on a juke-box. Do you find the same vividness throughout the poem?

CONSIDERING THE SNAIL is deceptively simple. The snail's passage is almost heroic. The poet cannot communicate with the snail, but he can celebrate its 'power'. As in other poems, Gunn admires strong will and 'purpose', however uncertain their outcome. These lines are in 'syllabic' metre, which means that each line (except the last) has seven syllables, but that there is no regular rhythm or rhyme. The pause at the end of the line imposes on the words a deliberation of tone which most fittingly reflects the movement of the snail. This slow, heavy movement is also enforced by the placing of two stressed syllables together. In 'snail pushes', 'green night', 'bright path', 'earth's dark', 'drenched there', and 'slow passion', the two emphasized syllables give a sense of deliberate, snail-like progress. Do you find anything incongruous in an heroic poem about a snail? Why do you imagine the poet chooses this theme?

ST. MARTIN AND THE BEGGAR. A modern ballad. It is an up-to-date version of one of the saints' legends that were so popular in the Middle Ages. Christ is reported as saying: 'In so far as ye have done it unto the least of these my brethren, ye have done it unto me.' What impression do you form of St. Martin?

A 'cenobite' is a young monk living in a community.

Discuss the moral ideas expressed by Martin in Stanzas 1 and 2, and by the transformed beggar in Stanzas 10 and 11. How far do they strike you as typically Christian?

SEAMUS HEANEY (1939–) pp. 77–78.

Brought up on a farm in Co. Derry. Educated at Queen's University, Belfast.

CHURNING DAY. A powerful physical quality is the most obvious characteristic of this poem. This is achieved by rhythmic and onomatopoeiac effects—'rhythms that slugged and thumped', 'the pat and slap of small spades on wet lumps'. The total effect is of a rich, coarse abundance, dominating, almost menacing, the house. The images of 'bombs' in the small pantry of 'coagulated sunlight', the comparison to a 'sulphur mine', all create this sense of natural power. The last four lines describe how the images of churning day, the completion of a natural process, become part of their brains, giving the family a sense of ease, a satisfaction, the clean symmetry of a crystal.

TED HUGHES (1930–) pp. 79–85.

Educated at Mexborough Grammar School, Yorkshire, and Pembroke College, Cambridge. Freelance writer and broadcaster.

THE HORSES. The poet walks early before dawn, and comes on a scene of horses. They are frozen and still, as if turned to stone. The word 'megalith' means a stone of great size, and the old Druid megaliths, at Stonehenge for instance, add an idea of religious awe and mystery to the word.

At dawn there is a great upsurge of energy, and the horses 'thaw'. They are still 'stone' and silent, but we have the sense of immanent rebirth. The poet's experience has the vividness of a dream, and the word 'fever' suggests something disturbing, even frightening, in the coming of life. But in memory, the experience is healing, like Wordsworth's moments of ecstatic experience. The horses are vividly etched on his mind. In the ordinary scenes of life, they come back with a promise of nature's vitality and endurance. The poet's imagery is extremely vivid and concrete, even though his experience is visionary. How does this vision compare with Edwin Muir's, in his poem with the same title (pp. 90–91).

SIX YOUNG MEN. The poet looks at a photograph of six young men who died in the world war of 1914–18. The photograph which 'holds them well' is also a reminder of their death; its celluloid has become 'faded and ochre-tinged' during their 'Forty years rotting into soil'. Hughes finds an agonizing paradox in the photograph, which shows these dead men with such an intensity of life. What do you think the last stanza means?

HAWK ROOSTING. Hughes lets his own human language speak for the godlike arrogance of the bird. The hawk's ruthlessness is both feared and admired. Unlike humans, he does not hide his cruelty in dreams, sophistries or polite manners. He represents the rule of kill or be killed, which civilized people pretend to condemn (but in fact obey?). Do you think a *man* might have the feelings of this hawk?

VIEW OF A PIG. Note the characteristic force of Hughes's syntax and imagery. He strives to convey the absolute quality of the pig's death—whatever life it once had is now unthinkable. The two penultimate stanzas are an inset; the poet remembers a piglet which he chased at a fair, and the energy of live pigs comes back to him. The last stanza is almost laconic in its failure to relate the two visions. Does the poem offer a moral, or a clear conclusion?

MY SISTER JANE. One of Ted Hughes's light-hearted poems, from *Meet My Folks*, a series of fantasies about his family.

PHILIP LARKIN (1922–) pp. 85–87.

Born in Coventry. In Oxford during the war. Now university librarian. Two novels—*Jill* and *A Girl in Winter*.

MYXOMATOSIS. A few years ago the disease, myxomatosis, killed most of the rabbits in this country. This was deliberately encouraged for purposes of pest control. 'Myxomatosis' appears a very simple poem, but it raises important questions. As in a trap, the rabbit is caught by pain. Larkin does not sentimentalize the situation. He kills the rabbit to end its agony, and the words 'clean my stick' show how unpleasant the experience is. He concludes by saying he's glad the rabbit cannot understand his suffering; it's easier not to have to explain that man is responsible. The carefully chosen words, the controlled rhythms and rhymes, are accurate and realistic. The simple monosyllables in the last line add to the sense of helplessness. Should men be allowed to interfere with nature in this way? Are they not caught in the same trap of suffering and death?

AT GRASS. The old racehorses in this poem are first seen lost in shadow, almost indistinguishable until the wind moves a tail or mane. The horses seem to be fading into death, and the simple words, rhymes and rhythm remind us of the pathos of old age and the swift passing of time. It's as if the horses were the shades of all human ambitions and triumphs. The pathos contrasts with the last stanza, in which Larkin expresses the freedom of the horses in their retirement. The poem contrasts the burdens of the race of life, colourful, briefly glorious, with the shadowy but unmolested life of withdrawal and retirement. At the end, as they are taken back to the stables, it's as if, in common with all men, they are submitting to death. Consider why the following words are so important to the poem: 'cold', 'anonymous', 'artificed', 'plague', 'unmolesting'.

MCMXIV. Presumably the poet is looking at a photograph of men queue-ing up to enlist in the 1914 War. The refrain, 'Never such innocence again', reminds us that the outbreak of the 1914 War produced an enor-mous imaginative shock. Many people had believed that such a war would never be possible in modern civilization. For Virginia Woolf, the novelist, the war came 'like a chasm in a smooth road'. Larkin creates the strange-ness of this pre-1914 society, already so far in the past that it seems out of a fairy-tale.

ALUN LEWIS (1915–1944) pp. 87–88.

Born at Aberdare. Educated at Cambridge Grammar School and Univer-sity College, Aberystwyth. Schoolteacher before the war. Officer in infantry, to India, 1943. Died on Arakan Front, 1944. Short story-writer.

ALL DAY IT HAS RAINED describes the boredom experienced by soldiers during the tedious periods of waiting that characterized the 1939–45 War. The long lines, words such as 'moody', 'dull', 'grey' and 'indiffer-ently', and the dominating image of rain, all suggest Lewis's sadness and weariness, a sense of inevitable movement towards the neutrality of death. Note the references to 'dream', as if in this monotony ordinary loves of past and future are irrelevant. In the last seven lines the children, the dog, and Edward Thomas the poet, have a beauty to oppose to the rain. But the poem ends with death—Thomas himself was killed in the 1914–18 War.

Do you find this at all similar to Edward Thomas's poems?

ROBERT LOWELL (1917–   ) pp. 88–89.

Born in Boston, Mass. Educated at St. Mark's School, Harvard, and Kenyon College. Conscientious objector during latter part of 1939–45 War and spent five months in a federal prison. University teacher.

WATER. This poem recaptures a moment of intimacy—the sort of happiness, sharp but elusive, which exists in the powerful concentrated images of a particular place. Maine is one of the States of the U.S.A. The 'white frame houses' are characteristic, and the poet feels a unity of land-scape, houses and sea. That 'Remember' in stanza 4 is beautifully judged —the tone of fond reminiscence. The dream in stanza 7 is ominous, the wish in stanza 8 futile. But memory recreates from them the vividness of things past. The poem is called WATER, and is a celebration of the sea. How does the word 'drenched' strike you? Does it suggest that water, fluid, a symbol of change, impregnates even the strongest objects like a rock? The sea is too 'cold' in the end for mortal men, but it is also refreshing. Is the poem's mood chiefly nostalgic? Sad? Happy?—

EDWIN MUIR (1887–1959) pp. 90–91.

Born and educated in the Orkneys. Well-known as critic and translator of Kafka.

THE HORSES. The search for knowledge has often been thought of as a from of evil pride. Man's distrust of modern science is embodied in the stories of Faustus and Frankenstein, and in much popular reaction to the atom bomb. The first part of this poem reminds us of the older myths. By his inventions, his radios and warships, tractors and planes, man has sacrificed himself to a mechanical world, and lost touch with his true nature. The result is a terrifying apocalypse. Muir's purpose is to describe a return to the lost Eden, a re-establishment of the old covenant with God. The seven days' war, which turns all to chaos, parodies God's creation of the world in seven days. Afterwards a simpler way of life is restored, with oxen and ploughs, until at last the horses can return to offer their 'long-lost archaic companionship'. The bond between man and Nature is restored.

Do you feel that this poem has anything in common with YOUR ATTENTION PLEASE by Peter Porter?

SYLVIA PLATH (1932–1963) pp. 91–95.

Born in Boston, Mass. Educated at Wellesley High School and Smith College. While on Fulbright scholarship to Newnham College, Cambridge, she met Ted Hughes, whom she married in 1956.

WATERCOLOUR OF GRANTCHESTER MEADOWS. Another poem about Grantchester—very different from Rupert Brooke's. This Grantchester is pretty and artificial, a pleasing miniature—'Nothing is big or far'. The whole scene is removed from harsh realities—the river 'bland', the cygnets 'tame', the meadows 'benign' and arcadian. The very water-rats are 'droll'. In Grantchester, students 'stroll or sit, hands laced, in a moony indolence of love'. The poet does not criticize, but her conclusion is a reminder of menaces surrounding the idyll: 'It is a country on a nursery plate.' In most of her poems, Sylvia Plath writes of Nature's bleaker moods.

POINT SHIRLEY. In this poem, Nature is wholly unlike the idyll of Grantchester. It is hard, uncompromising, and inflexibly opposed to the human will. The poet describes her American grandmother's life at

Point Shirley, her long battle against wind and sea. Now she is dead, and the elements resume their destruction: 'Steadily the sea Eats at Point Shirley.'

What reality has love—love which is a fight for survival and order against 'the sluttish, rutted sea'? The old woman 'died blessed', but the poet wonders how her love survives—'I would get from these dry-papped stones The milk your love instilled in them.' But 'though your graciousness might stream, And I contrive, Grandmother, stones are nothing of home...'

A bleak, powerful poem, typical of Sylvia Plath's sensibility in her early work.

MUSHROOMS. A sinister poem, reminiscent of science fiction. The creeping vegetation wills its survival after man has perished from the earth. The proliferation of the mushrooms is indefinably horrible—a life-force stripped of everything except the will to survive and multiply. Note the grim effectiveness of 'perfectly' in stanza 6, and the slimy humility of the mushrooms, especially in stanza 9. The form of life is depicted as ugly, mean, altogether inferior, a frightening reminder that the qualities we call 'higher'—intelligence, love, wisdom—may not be creation's final word.

The poem is in the form of mushroom *thoughts*, overheard or imagined. How acceptable do you find this?

PETER PORTER (1929–   ) pp. 95–96.

Born in Brisbane, Australia, his parents of English and Scottish origin. Came to England in 1951.

YOUR ATTENTION PLEASE. The poem depends for effect on its shock tactics, and in particular on exaggerations that are dangerously easy to believe. It has little verbal and rhythmic distinction, but may this be deliberate? The end of civilization is announced in *this* tone of voice. What is the tone? Who do you imagine the speaker to be?

THEODORE ROETHKE (1908–1963) pp. 97–99.

Born in Saginaw, Michigan. Educated at Michigan and Harvard. University teacher.

THE FAR FIELD. The man in late middle age, possibly close to death (section i), recollects a child's experience (section ii), and then moves on to thoughts of the future. In his experience, joy has prevailed over pain, and he journeys on gladly towards the adventure of death. Note how close the poet is to Nature, in his sympathy and vitality—Nature seems an extension of himself. Yet he is not *self*-centred. The 'I' in the poem has achieved detachment from self in response to a larger, freer world. Lying 'naked in sand', he has speculated light-heartedly on future reincarnation, as 'a snake or a raucous bird, Or, with luck, as a lion'. The waters which represent death are also symbols of freedom:

> I learned not to fear infinity,
> The far field, the windy cliffs of forever, . . .

And he says later: 'I am renewed by death, thought of my death.' This renewal is taken up in section iv, where the 'old man with his feet before the fire' is clothed in priestly robes 'of green, in garments of adieu'. In old age, the great, unanswered questions of life—'the why Of being born'—are felt again with exhilaration. The poem ends with mystical faith: 'All finite things reveal infinitude'; and with celebration of the beautiful world of transience which must now be transcended as the individual returns to the larger immensities.

This was one of Roethke's last poems, written towards the end of his life.

LOUIS SIMPSON (1923–) pp. 100–101.

Born in Jamaica. Moved to New York in 1940, and served with a U.S. airborne division in Europe. University teacher.

THE TROIKA. An exhilarating dream poem, as the Russian troika dashes from one romantic scene to the next—the greybeards bending over a game of chess, the girl combing her black hair, the white bird. Each scene recalls similar romantic scenes in other literature. We remember stories like that of the white bird which turns into a beautiful girl, or fairy-tales in which mysterious wise men are playing chess. Compare this poem with Auden's LADY, WEEPING AT THE CROSSROADS.

THE REDWOODS. On the West coast of America stand huge redwood trees hundreds of years old. This poem tries to create their mystery. Mountains are gradually being worn down by rivers, but the trees have a stillness that seems to be waiting for something—for a poet to be inspired by them, and to marry their beauty to his song.

GARY SNYDER (1930–) pp. 102–103.

Born in San Francisco. Educated at Reed College, Oregon, and University of California, Berkeley. One of leaders of the San Francisco Beat movement.

MID-AUGUST AT SOURDOUGH MOUNTAIN LOOKOUT. In the first stanza a series of images is given without grammatical connections. This allows the images to stand by themselves, without the poet introducing his own explanations and links. Snyder has spent much of his life on the West coast of the United States. He has a remarkable power of presenting its mountains, forests and streams in their own right, without imposing romantic subjective feelings. There is a simplicity and cleanness of the physical impressions here, which convey to us the wonder of the simplest experiences—drinking cold snow-water from a tin cup, or looking across rocks and meadows. And yet in this lyric the physical details take on a strange power. His own life, his reading and personal relationships, are forgotten as he looks down and celebrates the scene. Snyder is famous for his reverence for the world as it is, untainted by man's dreams and longings.

ABOVE PATE VALLEY celebrates the continued existence of man, over 10,000 years from primitive Indian to the contemporary trail-breaker. 'A small Green meadow watered by the snow, Edged with Aspen' is typical of the best of Snyder's images, full of simple pleasure in the things he sees. Compare these poems with those of W. H. Davies.

WILLIAM STAFFORD (1914–   ) p. 103.

Born in Kansas, U.S.A. Now teaches literature in an American College.

TRAVELLING THROUGH THE DARK concerns an incident on an American road. The traveller stops his car, because he sees a dead deer. There is a steep precipice beside the road, and if the dead animal is left there, a serious accident might be caused. The poet finds that the deer had been about to have a fawn, which is still alive in her body; but there is no way now in which it can be born.

The poet ends by pushing the dead animal over the precipice, as anyone else would, and driving on. The one difference is that he hesitates. Is this hesitation weakness, a simple failure to act with necessary ruthlessness? Or is it strength, an unusual sensitivity to death and suffering?

Note the contrast between the dead animal and the motor-car; note, too, that the poet feels as though the wilderness is listening for his decision. The phrase 'my only swerving' is a pun included for a serious purpose; the poet 'swerves' from normal behaviour by pausing to think, just as a motorist might 'swerve', if he saw a deer, and so kill himself and his passengers.

Consider the word 'more' in line 4. More *what?*

JON STALLWORTHY (1935–   ) pp. 104–105.

Educated at Rugby and Oxford. In the Royal West African Frontier Force. Publisher's editor, and literary critic.

NO ORDINARY SUNDAY. The poet begins by remembering the annual commemoration of the dead in the two world wars, as he experienced it at school. (A public school). He evokes the *feelings* of the Service, and his own response to the dead. In the last stanza, he moves—more briefly— to a memory of the same Sunday later in his life (now in the tropics).

What is the effect of juxtaposing two such memories? Does the poem develop an attitude to war and the 'heroic dead' that you could define? How do you think it compares with *either* Wilfred Owen's DULCE ET DECORUM EST *or* Ted Hughes's SIX YOUNG MEN?

IN THE STREET OF THE FRUIT STALLS. A richly glowing lyric, evoking an evening scene in the East. The last two lines deepen the exotic tone, with suggestions of a darker experience than the children understand.

DYLAN THOMAS (1914–1953) pp. 105–110.

Born in Swansea, Wales. Educated at Swansea Grammar School. Brief period as a newspaper reporter, then became famous after winning poetry contest in popular newspaper. Wrote short stories, and well-known radio play, *Under Milk Wood*. Highly successful poetry readings in America, 1950–53.

DO NOT GO GENTLE INTO THAT GOOD NIGHT. This villanelle is made up of five tercets, and a quatrain, all using only two rhymes. The first line is repeated at the end of the second and fourth tercet, the third line at the end of the third and fifth. The two repeated lines end the final quatrain. The form of the villanelle is difficult to handle, but Thomas loved verbal games. The repetitions give a feeling of ritual and ceremony to this prayer for Thomas's father, who died before the poem was published. The alliteration gives great drive and energy; the poem is written to be declaimed with passion.

The two rhyme words, light and night, stand for life and death. The poem is full of contradictions. 'Good night' suggests two things—a farewell, and yet also that death is 'good'. Thomas seems to be urging his father to rage against the approach of death, to refuse to give in, yet at the same time he says that death is 'good' because it is inevitable. Death is the natural end of life, and we must both accept this and yet rage against it.

Stanzas 2 to 5 consider different kinds of men—wise, good, wild and grave. Wise men are perhaps philosophers, who know that death is inevitable, 'dark is right'. They have never created poetry, with its power like forked lightning, and so, frustrated, they rage against death. Good men seems to mean puritans. They have avoided the dancing waters of the green bay of life, and so their frail deeds leave them also frustrated. Wild men are men of action, lovers of life, who learn too late that time passes and their happiness must be taken away. These three frustrated kinds of men contrast with 'grave' men, the poets of vision, like Yeats, who is recalled here (see his poem '*Lapis Lazuli*'). 'Grave' is a pun, meaning serious, but also recalling death, the grave. The poet is a 'grave' man who never forgets the truth of death. His 'blinding' sight is like the vision that came to Paul on the road to Damascus. He is blind to the temporary things of this world, but sees the vision.

And so the poem ends with a final contradiction, as Thomas asks his father both to curse and bless him. He must curse because the son has come to take his place; he must bless because this is a natural process. A poem in praise of life and in acceptance of death.

POEM IN OCTOBER. This poem was written in August 1944 as a celebration of Thomas's thirtieth birthday. In the first line, 'to heaven' may mean 'toward' or 'offered to'. Mainly it suggests that the journey of life is towards heaven. As he leaves the town, Laugharne, in the morning, he feels the holiness of Nature. The herons are priests, and the water is praying. There is a simple delight in physical impressions—the knock of boats on the wall, the call of seagull and rook. In the second stanza, as he passes 'Over the border', it's as if he's walked into another dimension. Above the clouds, he passes from rainy autumn into October sun, and suddenly he feels a confusion of the seasons—'A springful of larks', 'all the gardens Of spring and summer were blooming in the tall tales'. The 'tall tales' are his poems, where past and present interweave. 'The weather turned around' deliberately suggests confusion of weather, as if he's entered a region outside time.

Consider how the poem should be read aloud.

FERN HILL. Fern Hill is the home of Ann Jones, Thomas's aunt, where he went for holidays as a child. The poem is full of wonder and joy, the running, quick moving rhythms exhilarated and gay. In the first stanza, by taking the word 'lilting', which describes his own feelings, and applying it to the house, he suggests that the farm itself participates in his delight. There is a fairy-tale atmosphere in the opening 'Now as I was young and easy', and phrases like 'once below a time'. How does the poet arrive at such phrases? The words 'golden', 'prince', 'lordly' describe the glory he felt as a child. What are the precise suggestions?

This animated mood continues through the poem. At the end of the second stanza, 'slowly' gives a feeling of the long happy days of childhood, as he listens to the distant church bells; while 'holy' shows that for Thomas love of Nature is a religious experience. The third stanza beautifully creates the boy's tired mind, falling to sleep with the movements of the farm still part of his consciousness. Fern Hill is like Eden, 'after the birth of the simple light'. But there are also hints that this joy is not permanent. Time lets him play, he is heedless, and so, as we approach the end of the poem, he contrasts his careless happiness with his awakening into adult life. But there is no nostalgia here. He celebrates the innocent wonder of the child, young and easy under the temporary mercies of time.

Consider the tone of the last stanza. Is it sad, or still joyful? Do you get a strong impression of what the speaker of the poem was like as a man?

R. S. THOMAS (1913–) pp. 110–112.

Educated at the University of Wales and St. Michael's College, Llandaff. Ordained deacon 1936, priest 1937. Rector of Manafon, 1942–54. Vicar of St. Michael's Eglwysfach, 1954.

ABERSOCH. Abersoch is in North Wales, a very beautiful stretch of beach looking southwards to Harlech. The poet records a strong mood which comes upon him one evening in the calm before thunder. The question he asks (lines 9–11) has no answer, except in other questions (lines 12–14), tentative and inconclusive. Yet the mood is vividly evoked. Compare this poem with Edward Thomas's ADLESTROP. What similarities strike you? What differences?

A BLACKBIRD SINGING. Again, a moment's mood. The poet hears a blackbird singing, and responds to its unexpectedness. Why does he begin: 'It seems wrong ...'? Try to define the poet's feelings. Is he chiefly happy or sad? What do you understand by 'history's overtones'? Try to define the effect of the words 'black' and 'dark' in this poem.

THE COUNTRY CLERGY. The poet thinks of the dedicated, withdrawn lives of the country clergy, who have died leaving no literary memorial to 'their lonely thought In grey parishes'. Does he make their lives seem attractive? Valuable? Wasted? Consider the emotional force of the sentence beginning 'And yet their skulls' ... Do you feel that the poet despises the 'oafs and yokels'? Consider the words 'Too soon forgotten'. Does this suggest complete pessimism? Try to assess the emotional flavour of the poem's conclusion.

ON THE FARM. Note the fairy-tale quality—three brutish brothers, and the sister: 'Beauty under some spell of the beast.' But the poem is far from being a fairy-tale. It is a close, unsentimental look at a Welsh hillside home. The images suggest violence (line 5) and disgust (line 10). It is as though a blight has fallen on Nature (lines 13–15). Yet the poem moves towards religious affirmation, reached through deprivation and despair.

The last two lines are among the most profound and astonishing in any poem included in this book. The sense of a winter world is caught in that wholly unexpected, wholly inescapable 'shrill'.

CHARLES TOMLINSON (1927–   ) pp. 112–113.

Educated at Queen's College, Cambridge, and the University of London. University teacher.

SNOW SEQUENCE. Tomlinson tries to efface himself completely from this poem, and to register objects and scenes precisely. He records every detail minutely, satisfied with depicting things as they are.

Do you find the poem effective?

JOHN WAIN (1925–   ) pp. 113–116.

Educated at the High School, Newcastle-under-Lyme, and St. John's College, Oxford. At first university lecturer at Reading. Now freelance novelist and critic.

ON THE DEATH OF A MURDERER. At the start our sympathies are with the hunted man; only later do we discover who he is. Wain writes of the moment when a Nazi killer is run to earth, and when society has to deal with him. Should he be killed, as he has killed? Or should he be treated with mercy and love? The human cycle of revenge and bloodshed is explored in this poem, which 'explains' the Nazi's behaviour without excusing it. In the end the killer dies, but his curse is perpetuated. Modern war is seen as a deadly infection. Only in the last line does the healing word 'love' appear.

Do you think that the murderer should have been forgiven?

THIS ABOVE ALL IS PRECIOUS AND REMARKABLE. A poem that reminds us that not all modern writers are cynical or extremist. The dignity of the opening line, its resonance, is carried throughout the poem.

ACKNOWLEDGEMENTS

We wish to thank the following for permission to reprint copyright poems:

W. H. Auden:	Faber and Faber Ltd.
John Betjeman:	John Murray (Publishers) Ltd.
E. E. Cummings:	Faber & Faber Ltd. and Harcourt Brace and World Inc. © 1926 by Horace Liveright renewed 1954 by E. E. Cummings
W. H. Davies:	Mrs. H. M. Davies and Jonathan Cape Ltd.
Walter de la Mare:	The Society of Authors and Richard de la Mare
Keith Douglas:	Faber & Faber Ltd.
T. S. Eliot:	Faber & Faber Ltd.
D. J. Enright:	David Higham Associates
Robert Frost:	Laurence Pollinger Limited
Karen Gershon:	Victor Gollancz Ltd.
Robert Graves:	A. P. Watt & Son
Thom Gunn:	Faber & Faber Ltd.
Thomas Hardy:	Macmillan & Co. Ltd.
Seamus Heaney:	Faber and & Faber Ltd.
Ted Hughes:	Faber & Faber Ltd.
Philip Larkin:	The Marvell Press and Faber & Faber Ltd.
D. H. Lawrence:	Laurence Pollinger Ltd. and The Estate of the late Mrs. Frieda Lawrence
Alun Lewis:	George Allen & Unwin Ltd.
Robert Lowell:	Faber & Faber Ltd.
Archibald MacLeish:	Houghton Mifflin Company
Louis MacNeice:	Faber & Faber Ltd.
Edwin Muir:	Faber & Faber Ltd.
Ogden Nash:	J. M. Dent & Sons Ltd.
Wilfred Owen:	Harold Owen and Chatto & Windus Ltd.
Sylvia Plath:	Miss Olwyn Hughes
Peter Porter:	Scorpion Press
Ezra Pound:	Faber & Faber Ltd.
Theodore Roethke:	Faber & Faber Ltd.
Seigfried Sassoon:	The Author
Louis Simpson:	Oxford University Press
Gary Snyder:	Fulcrum Press
Stephen Spender:	Faber & Faber Ltd.
William Stafford:	Harper & Row © 1960 from *Travelling Through the Dark*
John Stallworthy:	Oxford University Press from *Out of Bounds*
Dylan Thomas:	J. M. Dent & Sons
Edward Thomas:	Mrs. Myfanwy Thomas
R. S. Thomas:	Rupert Hart-Davis Ltd.
Charles Tomlinson:	Oxford University Press
John Wain:	Macmillan & Co. Ltd.
W. B. Yeats:	A. P. Watt & Son

Index of First Lines